CORPORATE INTERIORS

No.5

CORPORATE INTERIORS
No.5

Edited by
Roger Yee

Visual Reference Publications Inc., New York

Visual Reference Publications Inc.
302 Fifth Avenue
New York, NY 10001

Distributors to the trade in the United States and Canada
Watson-Guptill
770 Broadway
New York, NY 10003

Distributors outside the United States and Canada
HarperCollins International
10 East 53rd Street
New York, NY 10022-5299

Library of Congress Cataloging in Publication Data:
Corporate Interiors No.5

Printed in China
ISBN 1-58471-031-4

Book design: Harish Patel Design Associates
Book production: John Hogan
Printing by: C&C Offset Printing, Hong Kong

Contents

Introduction

How is Corporate America preparing for economic recovery? Look at its workplaces.

This is the fifth annual volume of a book that was conceived to answer three critical questions: What does Corporate America look like? Who makes it look that way? Why does it look that way? A bumper crop of books and magazines keeps everyone well informed on what's happening in residential design. By contrast, there has been no annual reference volume—until this book made its debut—offering a timely, diverse and comprehensive overview of the latest developments in the design of office environments for businesses and institutions.

But we're living in uncertain times, some might say. Who can think about new office space in the face of economic stagnation, political instability, and public health scares? Why not wait for better days?

Good times or bad, corporate executives appreciate this book the moment they discover the needs of their organizations are no longer being met by their facilities. Since few executives know how to develop office interiors, much less entire corporate campuses, they quickly acknowledge the risks of creating a new work environment by searching for an appropriate architect or interior designer. Which design firm will most effectively promote the corporate interests? How are the best design firms identified, where do they practice, and what is the nature of their work?

Executives should keep in mind that there is more than meets the eye in the 186 projects chosen for publication by the 49 participating firms in Corporate Interiors No. 5. Yes, these installations are exceptional in appearance. Nevertheless, efficient space plans, state-of-the-art power, voice and data services, high quality lighting, acoustics, air quality and ergonomics, and versatile workplace furnishings and total environments are what make them truly outstanding. Good design is good business because it allows people to perform at their best.

Of course, good design is also subject to the shifting cultural tastes of the moment. The post-dot-com, post-September 11, post-Iraqi war world has taken us to a far more risk-averse and serious-minded place than readers might recall from the first four volumes of Corporate Interiors. Yet the projects that appear on the following pages should reassure us that corporate America has learned some vital lessons from the dot-com boom years about how workplaces really function. For example, status and hierarchy are natural sources of expression in office design, but job tasks are more practical and cost-effective. Or creative exchanges of ideas are likely to occur in informal meeting places, so facilities like cappuccino bars should be provided along with conference rooms and the like.

To give you an idea of the resources available for your project, the book furnishes a project-by-project listing of the manufacturers whose products have been specified for their clients by the architects and interior designers in Corporate Interiors No. 5. This is followed by additional information from companies whose products may merit serious consideration by you and your design firm. As you prepare to develop new facilities for your organization, remember that you can truly achieve as much as you are willing to devote to your project in terms of time, resources and serious involvement between the people of your organization and the consultants of your design team.

Lester Dundes
Publisher

AREA

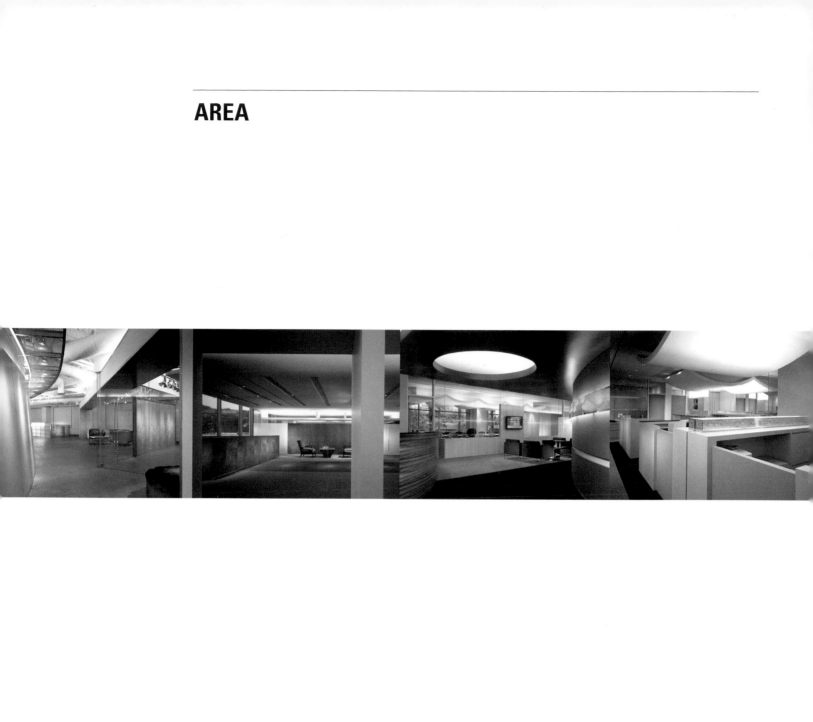

550 South Hope Street
18th Floor
Los Angeles
California 90071
213.623.8909
213.623.4275 (Fax)
info@areaarchitecture.com

Spectacular Pacific Ocean views represent just one reason for Beacon Pictures's recent move from Hollywood to Santa Monica's Ocean Boulevard. Nevertheless, the sea's presence is felt in the new, 18,000-square foot facility, designed by AREA, for 30 employees of the independent motion picture company founded in 1990 by producer Armyan Bernstein to make such films as Spy Game, Bring It On, The Hurricane, and Air Force One. From the reception area, a broad, curved and canted wall directs the flow of traffic to the office wing, containing private and open-plan offices and the executive suite, or the public wing, which accommodates meetings and receptions. To acknowledge the client's wish for a "rough and ready" image of filmmaking and timeless sophistication, exposed building systems are dramatically juxtaposed with elegant materials and furnishings—and the sea.

Above left: Private office.

Above right: View from reception to offices.

Left: Open-plan work area.

Opposite: Reception.

Photography: Jon Miller/ Hedrich Blessing.

Right: Conference room.

Below left: Reception.

Below right: Open work stations.

Photography: Jon Miller/ Hedrich Blessing.

Making high-profile show business clients feel comfortable is a legitimate concern for the entertainment law firm of Lichter, Grossman, Nichols, Adler & Goodman that extends throughout its new, 10,000-square foot Los Angeles office, designed by AREA. The space overlooks a splendid view of the Hollywood Hills. Accordingly, the interior design extends the deep indoors to benefit company employees and their clients through such means as translucent glass panels set below clear glass clerestories in corridor walls, and indirectly illuminated light shelves that project a soft glow on ceilings, motifs that shape the conference rooms, private attorneys' offices and open assistants' work stations. It's a unique workplace, fulflling partner Peter Nichols's demanding goals.

AREA

O'Melveny & Myers LLP
Irvine, California

Above: Reception.

Left: Open secretarial area.

Opposite: Conference room.

Photography: Jon Miller/ Hedrich Blessing.

How do you convey the rich history of the oldest Los Angeles-based law firm, one of the region's largest, in a satellite location serving the growing, high-tech economy of Orange County? For O'Melveny & Myers, the development of its new, 12,000-square foot Irvine office for 30 employees, designed by AREA, can be seen as a bold look forward in time and a fond evocation of southern California culture. The front area of a space divided by an exit corridor includes conference rooms with advanced audio-visual systems, an interactive library with flat screen monitors and wireless keyboards, lounge-style conferencing rooms, and an open area with movable glass screens that can be reconfigured for various public functions. By contrast, the back area resembles a Beverly Hills talent agency designed by AREA and toured by representatives of O'Melveny & Myers—a setting that's advanced in its organization-

al dynamics, nonetheless. Glass-fronted private offices flank an open secretarial corridor on both sides, creating an egalitarian situation for sharing natural light and views and supporting teamwork that is uncommon in traditional law offices. Other creative touches, such as lighting fixtures featuring curved neon tubes shielded by perforated stainless steel, draped drywall ceiling pads that diffuse light, suspended soffits with cove-lighted ocu-luses, and contemporary, European-style furnishings keep this over-110-year-old firm from showing its age in youthful Orange County.

Aref & Associates Design Studio

100 N. Sepulveda Boulevard
Suite 100
El Segundo
California 90245
310.414.1000
310.414.1099 (Fax)
www.aref.com
faaref@aref.com
mharef@aref.com

Aref & Associates Design Studio

Aref & Associates Design Studio

Vivendi Universal Interactive Publishing
Los Angeles, California

With the structure and content of the media world changing continuously, visitors at the striking and recently completed, 7,300-square foot Los Angeles office for 30 employees of Vivendi Universal Interactive Publishing, designed by Aref & Associates Design Studio, should be intrigued by what awaits them. At this video games operation of Vivendi Universal, the French media conglomerate, the facility combines contemporary office functions with fresh ideas about collaborative, team-based work to give employees an open, informal and interactive workplace. Here a conventional office planning grid is put to work creating unconventional private offices, teaming work stations, conference rooms, team rooms and computer room, and such amenities as a cafe-style commons and original art and other amenities. It's just the kind of setting, infused with fresh, contemporary furnishings, vibrant original artwork and dramatic lighting, that seems to say "stay tuned" to youthful audiences—including the Vivendi employees, who love their space—which just happens to be the media world's mantra of the moment.

Right: Cafe.

Below: Reception.

Opposite upper right: Open plan work stations.

Opposite lower left: Corridor at elevator lobby.

Photography: Paul Bielenberg.

Aref & Associates Design Studio

Kilroy Realty Corporation
Los Angeles, California

Above: Open-plan office space.
Left: Reception.
Below left: Board room.
Photography: Michael Parker.

It's immediately apparent from the refined appearance of the new office of Kilroy Realty Corporation in Los Angeles, designed by Aref & Associates Design Studio, that the company founded in 1947 by chairman John B. Kilroy, Sr. knows its business. The accommodations including private offices, open-plan work areas, conference rooms, reception and support services, are simultaneously well organized, equipped with the latest office technologies and sleekly tailored in a clean, modern style. Kilroy, a fully integrated real estate enterprise that has been active for five decades in the commercial office and industrial property markets of the western United States, primarily California, has an exceptional workplace for its next five decades.

Aref & Associates Design Studio

Allen Matkins Leck Gamble & Mallory, LLP
Los Angeles, California

If commitment to quality is the main reason behind the growth of Allen Matkins Leck Gamble & Mallory in its first 25 years as a law firm, during which it expanded to over 200 lawyers in five major California business centers, the same commitment is evident in its new, 25,000-square foot office for 80 employees in Los Angeles, designed by Aref & Associates Design Studio. The private attorneys' offices, secretarial work stations, conference rooms, war rooms and computer room have created an airy, open and inviting environment that Allen Matkins, which has a strong real estate practice, is now showcasing it to the real estate community.

Top: Reception and main conference room.

Above: Secretarial work stations.

Left: View from elevator lobby.

Photography: Paul Bielenberg.

21

Aref & Associates Design Studio

Aref & Associates Design Studio
El Segundo, California

Right: Conference room.
Lower right: Studio.
Opposite above: Library.
Opposite below: Reception.
Photography: Paul Bielenberg.

Since Aref & Associates Design Studio was founded to meet the space planning and interior design needs of major corporations, professional service firms and real estate developers, its handsome, new, 8,000-square foot office for 16 employees in El Segundo, California has been developed like a visual prospectus to be read by current and prospective clients. The interior design is attractive, cost effective and conducive to creative work, reflecting the concerns of many business executives and principals of professional organizations. Yet its private offices, teaming work stations, conference rooms, team rooms, commons and reception are anything but generic in appearance. The firm attributes its success as a boutique design firm to the collaborative effort of its design team as well as its principals' commitment to a hands-on approach to planning and design, and its new office confidently proclaims a willingness to follow its own counsel.

Aref & Associates Design Studio

Red Bull North America, Inc.
Santa Monica, California

Ever grab a Red Bull by the horns? Many U.S. devotees of extreme sports already enjoy this European energy soft drink, thanks to its sponsorship of lifestyle events. To handle the brand's impressive growth, the company has developed a new, 23,000-square foot office in Santa Monica, California, designed for 700 employees by Aref & Associates Design Studio. The clean, European look of the private offices, teaming workspace, conference rooms, team rooms, computer room and commons should give Red Bull plenty of room to run.

Above: Reception.

Left: View towards conference room.

Right: Row of private offices.

Photography: Paul Bielenberg.

Bergmeyer Associates, Inc.

Bergmeyer Associates, Inc.
Architecture and Interiors
286 Congress Street
Boston, MA 02210
617.542.1025
617.338.6897 (Fax)
www.bergmeyer.com
info@bos.bergmeyer.com

Bergmeyer Associates, Inc.

NerveWire
Newton, Massachusetts

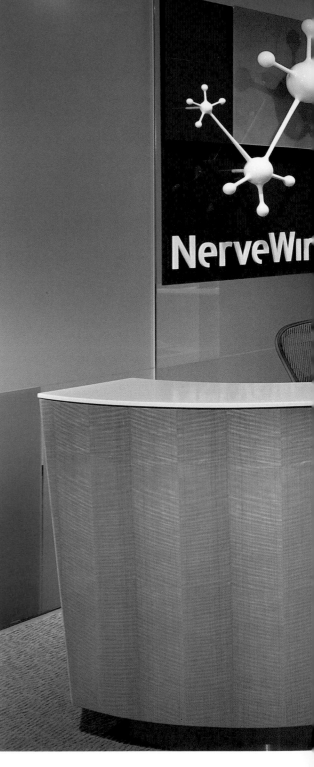

Above: Circulation and informal meeting spaces.

Right: Reception area.

Below left: Typical team room.

How do you satisfy an organization whose needs embrace public forums and intimate places, openness and privacy, team effort and individual tasks, and new and old economy clients—while reinforcing its brand and supporting its team-based delivery of services? This was the challenge posed by NerveWire at the company's new, 54,000-square foot, three-level office for 244 employees. To fulfill its complex requirements for the workplace, Bergmeyer carefully structured the high-tech environment to achieve a dynamic balance among contrasting conditions. As a result, private offices, open work spaces, project team rooms, formal and informal meeting areas, training room, computer rooms, kitchens/dining

spaces, and game room
offer employees countless
spatial options whatever
their assignment may be.

Right: Waiting area for
reception.

Photography: Lucy Chen.

Bergmeyer Associates, Inc.

CGN
Boston, Massachusetts

Above: Circulation.
Above right: Conference room.
Below: Meeting area.
Photography: Lucy Chen.

Natural light floods the 13,750-square foot office of CGN, a marketing and creative services firm in Boston, Massachusetts—adding form, color and drama to a spare yet warm modern environment. Designed by Bergmeyer, the simplicity is in keeping with the client's program for this project, and marries well with the re-use of existing built elements. The designer introduced "light fins" at conference rooms to provide visual privacy from the lobby and allow natural light to bathe the corridor. Birch framed translucent screens and doors were introduced as a motif to give enclosure to workstations while extending vistas throughout the entire office for this 55-person marketing communications company. Indirect and recessed lighting fixtures, coupled with exterior light, illuminate walls in the private offices, open plan workstations and conference rooms. The reception/waiting area with its light maple woods and translucent screens includes an understated coffee bar where CGN serves such clients as Amtrak, Fidelity Investments, Massachusetts Office of Travel & Tourism and Salomon Smith Barney. An understated use of strong geometry, long and short views and a simple but warm color palette give the space its sophisticated but casually cool tone.

Bergmeyer Associates, Inc.

Intex Solutions, Inc.
Needham, Massachusetts

It's one thing to fall in love with a warehouse. It's another to transform one at a Needham, Massachusetts office park into a 23,000-square foot office for 70 employees of Intex, a provider of timely and comprehensive data, models and related software for the structured fixed-income market. Because Intex wanted to retain the warehouse space, Bergmeyer rotated the floor plan 45 degrees to the building grid. The private offices and custom work stations of departments, product assembly, computer and conference rooms are gathered around a central skylit "piazza", much like a medieval Italian city. Custom freestanding screens used instead of furniture system panels, a garage door that expands the main conference room, and the landscaped "piazza" for informal meetings and dining are special features that give Intex one truly exceptional warehouse.

Right: Open plan work stations with screens.

Below: Exterior.

Bottom: Reception.

Below right: Piazza.

Photography: Lucy Chen.

Bergmeyer Associates, Inc.

Lehman Millet Incorporated
Boston, Massachusetts

Right: The lunch room and kitchen with ceramic glass cooktop.

Below right: President Bruce Lehman's office overlooking the atrium.

Below left: The atrium stair. The kitchen is visible on the upper level.

Opposite page: LMI's conference room is dubbed "the garage."

Photography: Lucy Chen.

This renovation of a historic mercantile building in Boston's Bulfinch Triangle was designed for the 60 employees of Lehman Millet Incorporated (LMI), a medical marketing communications firm. It occupies three floors of approximately 7,000 sq. ft. each. For all its history, the building had the disadvantage of a long plan with windows only along the two narrow ends; this the designers alleviated by inserting a central skylit atrium that contains a new cantilevered stair of structural steel with concrete treads. The rest of space was gutted to the basic structural elements: brick bearing walls, some of which have been left exposed and painted white; wood joist floor systems, and a central row of structural columns, cast iron on the lower floors and wood on the upper floors. The main lobby introduces the new materials that are used throughout: galvanized sheet steel, blonde sycamore paneling, white Surell solid surfacing material by Formica, and black terrazzo. The offices of LMI's president Bruce Lehman and chairman Gerry Millet look out to the atrium on the

next-to-top floor, putting them at the heart of the company's activity. On the floor above, beneath a peaked roof with multiple skylights, are two of the facility's most unusual spaces; the first is a large conference room that can be enclosed with a pair of anodized aluminum and glass garage doors and that is affectionately nicknamed "the garage"; the second,

nearby, is a lunchroom and kitchen with a ceramic glass cooktop anchored to a stainless steel work island; above the island is a suspended stainless steel pot rack designed by chairman Millet himself. Indirect light in the workspaces is complemented by track lighting in the public areas, and furnishings throughout are resolutely modern.

Above: View from conference room toward reception area.

Right: Main lobby.

Photography: Lucy Chen.

Brayton + Hughes Design Studio

639 Howard Street
San Francisco
California 94105
415.291.8100
415 434 8145 (Fax)
www@bhdstudio.com
info@bhdstudio.com

Brayton + Hughes Design Studio

DFS Group Limited
Corporate Headquarters
San Francisco, California

Long before airports became retail centers, DFS or Duty Free Shoppers turned airline passengers into shoppers, starting with a liquor, tobacco, cosmetic and fragrance duty-free concession at the Hong Kong airport in 1961. Today, as part of French conglomerate LVMH, DFS Group Limited operates over 150 luxury retail stores in 15 countries throughout Asia and the Pacific Basin, staffed by some 5,000 employees. The new, 110,000-square foot, four-floor corporate headquarters in San Francisco, designed by Brayton + Hughes Design Studio, serves as a backdrop for DFS Group's specialty shop merchandise, the sleek private and open-plan offices, boardroom, training room, product development and display facilities, lunchroom, coffee/copy rooms and limestone feature stair resemble showcases themselves. Accented in a subtle Asian theme to acknowledge the retailer's Asian markets using hardwoods, stone, plaster, frosted glass and fabric, and illuminated by a sophisticated blend of daylight, Bay Area views, halogen lighting fixtures for display, and ambient pendant lighting fixtures for computer work, the interiors look good enough to take home.

Above: Reception.
Below left: Open-plan area.
Below right: Boardroom.
Opposite: Vignette in reception.
Photography: John Sutton.

Brayton + Hughes Design Studio

Morrison & Foerster
San Francisco, California

Top: Perimeter office.

Above: Reception.

Right: Lounge in conference center.

Opposite: Conference room.

Photography: John Sutton

One of the world's largest law firms with 1,000 lawyers in 18 offices, Morrison & Foerster can move swiftly in response to clients seeking greater service at reduced overhead cost. A good example is its new, 153,000-square foot, six-floor office in San Francisco, designed by Brayton + Hughes Design Studio. The space supports flexible, team-based work methodologies instead of traditional organizational hierarchies. Modular perimeter offices feature shared conference space between partner and associate offices, reception and conference facilities are centralized for efficiency and security, and flexible interior support zones and work rooms with shared storage lockers serve multiple cases. Every detail counts: Circulation concentrates at the building core to ease traffic adjacent to private offices and work areas.

Brayton + Hughes Design Studio

Boyd Lighting Company
San Francisco, California

An aging yet rugged concrete and steel industrial building would seem an unlikely place to find the newest concepts in modern lighting fixtures. However, visitors to the 11,000-square foot showroom, gallery and office space, designed by Brayton + Hughes Design Studio, that serves as the headquarters of Boyd Lighting Company in San Francisco are not disappointed by what they find. The modern, multi-level interior, virtually reconstructed for seismic stability, combines space, daylight and artificial light to maximize interaction between certain departments, establish privacy for others, and provide a large showroom space that is dark enough to maintain control of various lighting scenarios. This complex balancing act is achieved through a skillful manipulation of building elements, not the least of which are Boyd's handsome lighting fixtures.

Above left: Upper level cafe.
Below left: Exterior.
Below right: Reception desk.
Opposite: Main corridor.
Photography: John Sutton.

Brayton + Hughes Design Studio

San Francisco Loft
San Francisco, California

A converted 19th-century warehouse at the foot of the San Francisco Bay Bridge in San Francisco has become the setting for a new and neatly tailored, 1,500-square foot, two-floor live/work loft space, designed by Brayton + Hughes Design Studio. What the client sought was an office/meeting space and file archive that could double as a weekend pied á terre. The resulting design, which features a wall of maple casework holding aluminum file boxes, an opposing wall with a sofa and a pair of lounge chairs, pine flooring and track lighting, revolves around a curving, maple-paneled hinged wall that opens to disclose a kitchen of concrete and galvanized steel. Two comfortable bedrooms and baths, discreetly tucked away upstairs, complete this appealing scheme.

Above: Hinged wall encloses kitchen.

Below left: Seating area, kitchen and stairs to living quarters.

Below right: Archive wall of maple casework.

Photography: John Sutton.

Burt Hill Kosar Rittelmann Associates

270 Congress Street
Boston, MA 02210
617.423.4252
617.423.4333 (Fax)

400 Morgan Center
Butler, PA 16001
724.285.4761
724.285.6815 (Fax)

1735 Market Street
53rd Floor
Philadelphia, PA 19103
215.751.2900
215.751.2901 (Fax)

650 Smithfield Street
Suite 2600
Pittsburgh, PA 15222
412.394.7000
412.394.7880 (Fax)

1056 Thomas Jefferson Street NW
Washington, DC 20007
202.333.2711
202.333.3159 (Fax)

1 Chagrin Highlands
2000 Auburn Drive
Suite 200
Beachwood, OH 44122
216.378.7840
216.378.7841 (Fax)

www.burthill.com

Burt Hill Kosar Rittelmann Associates

Blattner Brunner, Inc.
Pittsburgh, Pennsylvania

"Change the way you think" is more than a motto at Blattner Brunner. The progressive Pittsburgh advertising agency did just that for its innovative, new, 38,000-square foot, two-level office, designed by Burt Hill Kosar Rittelmann Associates. The open environment centers on Town Square, a large, mixed-use area with coffee bar, informal seating and interconnecting stair. Whether the 148 employees gather there or at open-plan work stations, privacy rooms, meeting rooms, creative library or kitchens, they have countless options for interaction and collaboration. "We do a lot of things differently because of the way our space is designed," notes Joe Blattner, CEO.

Above: Upper level of connecting stair.

Right: Entry with concierge.

Far right: Small conference room.

Opposite: Town Square and connecting stair.

Photography: Ed Massery.

Burt Hill Kosar Rittelmann Associates

Xplorion
Pittsburgh, Pennsylvania

Looking for places in southwestern Pennsylvania to open new businesses or expand existing operations? The task has become a lot more enticing following the recent completion of Xplorion, a 3,300-square foot, interactive media showcase created for Pittsburgh

Regional Alliance Business Resource Center, with interactive media display areas, virtual theater and meeting areas designed by Burt Hill Kosar Rittelmann Associates. Xplorion attracts business people, tourists and residents alike thanks to the skillful way its design inte-

grates a wide variety of specialized environments on different elevations into a continuous spatial experience that is exciting to behold and easy to navigate. The space, equipped with a custom access floor, multi-layered ceiling, bold, modern forms and dramatic lighting, has

become the favored marketing venue for the region's economic development agencies, drawing 11,000 visitors in its first year.

Above left: A view towards the street level entrance.

Left: XplorionConnect, an array of six user-friendly digital kiosks.

Exhibit design: Agnew Moyer Smith.

Photography: Craig Thompson.

44

Above: XplorionInvision, a video wall featuring 10 gas plasma flat screens, left, and XplorionQuest, a virtual theater, right.

Left: XplorionQuest, a 12-seat spherical virtual theater offering simulated flights of the region.

45

Burt Hill Kosar Rittelmann Associates

Spang & Company
Pittsburgh, Pennsylvania

Above: Break area.

Below left: Internal stair in reception.

Below right: Periphery open-plan area.

Bottom right: Employee rest-room.

Opposite: Reception.

Photography: Edward Massery.

When Spang & Company relocated its headquarters 90 miles to Pittsburgh from Butler, Pennsylvania, the move precipitated major changes for the privately held, $100-million-plus manufacturing business founded in 1894 as a machine shop servicing Pennsylvania's oil fields. Besides adding a new commute for established employees, the new, 32,000-square foot, two-level facility, designed by Burt Hill Kosar Rittelmann Associates, has introduced the 56 employees to open offices for the first time. The result is a technologically advanced and user-friendly environment that is light, open and comfortable, with most constructed elements located towards the core, partial-height work station panels and full-height partitions kept low to transmit daylight, sound masking technology managing the acoustics, and visual interest enhanced by varied ceiling planes, indirect and accent lighting, and a material vocabulary accented by granite, metal and glass. "We're seeing response to our new facilities," reports Frank Rath, Spang's CEO, "in terms of both productivity and appreciation of our workplace amenities."

Burt Hill Kosar Rittelmann Associates

Ketchum
Pittsburgh, Pennsylvania

Above left: Coffee bar.

Above right: Teaming area.

Below left: Reception.

Below right: Informal conference room.

Photography: Edward Massery.

Like other busy organizations, the Pittsburgh office of Ketchum, one of the world's leading public relations agencies, wanted to renovate and expand its occupied offices without skipping a day's work—a major challenge for obvious reasons. However, Burt Hill Kosar Rittelmann Associates has successfully completed a seven-phase project that updates the 72,300-square foot, three-floor space housing 258 employees with the latest technology and management concepts. From the private and open-plan offices and conference center to the new teaming areas, Ketchum has a new outlook on life.

48

Callison Architecture, Inc.

1420 Fifth Avenue
Suite 2400
Seattle, WA 98101
206.623.4646
206.623.4625 (Fax)
www.callison.com

Callison Architecture, Inc.

Orrick, Herrington, Sutcliffe LLP
Menlo Park Office
Menlo Park, California

During the peak of the dot.com boom, the Menlo Park, California office of Orrick, Herrington & Sutcliffe quietly accomplished what others might have considered possible only in virtual reality. The key to the redesign of this Silicon Valley, full-service, 650-employee, law firm was to attract and retain the best legal talent, project an image as the best law firm for clients and attorneys, create a range of formal and informal meeting spaces, and reduce the size of private offices for partners and associates while increasing their comfort, utility and sheer numbers. To pull off this feat, Callison Architecture made innovative use of 43,000 square feet in a new office building to accommodate not only the more than 50 employees assigned there, but also employees housed in an existing, nearby but unconnected facility. A design theme drawing on the qualities of water as a serene, quietly powerful and forever changing state of matter became the inspiration for private offices that are angled and furnished with appropriately scaled and flexible furniture, compact but well planned meeting spaces, a consolidated conference center for all employees, a multi-functional space for socializing, a village green, and on-site dining. The handsome environment has earned the equivalent of countless Silicon Valley double-clicks from clients and attorneys alike.

Below left: Conference area.

Below right: Coffee bar, a social "eddy" in corridor.

Opposite: Lobby.

Photography: Chris Eden.

Callison Architecture, Inc..

Orrick, Herrington, Sutcliffe LLP
Seattle Office
Seattle, Washington

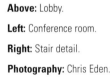

How did a 135-plus-year-old law firm from San Francisco properly enter the Seattle market? For Orrick, the solution lay in working with Callison Architecture to develop a 48,000-square-foot space for over 50 employees that balanced elegance and sophistication. To appeal to a wider market of both international and corporate intellectual property clients, the design became a mix of Pacific Rim, multi-cultural influences and a crisp, stylish, aesthetic. Yet decisions to promote views and interaction by breaking down barriers, vary the mood by using wood and glass, and maximizing clients' time by creating inviting group spaces with movable furniture, data/power connections and plasma screens transform this award-winning design into considerably more.

Above: Lobby.
Left: Conference room.
Right: Stair detail.
Photography: Chris Eden.

Callison Architecture, Inc.

Future@Work II
Seattle, Washington

French visionary Jules Verne could have said it as well as anyone: The future is not what it used to be. Nevertheless, Future@Work II is a fascinating, 3,000-square foot workplace in Seattle where Callison Architecture has evolved its thinking about how to effectively sustain today's office workers beyond Future@Work, which opened in 1997. In addition, the prototype space proposes accommodations for businesses at every stage of development from seed to growth to maturity to provide the most amount of resources for adaptability and flexibility. Highlights of Future@Work II's 11 key areas include: The Immersion Space, an interactive war room, The Dorm, Harbor and Study, three approaches to private space, and The Media Lounge, an informal, user-configured meeting area. The future looks promising, indeed.

Callison Architecture, Inc.

HQ
Portland, Oregon, New York, New York, Waltham, Massachusetts and Other Locations

Think about how often businesses are born in garages—like Hewlett Packard, Walt Disney Company, Goodyear and Apple Computer—and you'll readily perceive the value of HQ Global Workplaces, the nation's largest provider of office outsourcing. Addison, Texas-based HQ, which has rented furnished, staffed and state-of-the-art offices to businesses for over 30 years, recently retained Callison Architecture and a multi-disciplinary team of workplace consultants, retail designers and branding experts to redefine the executive suites industry. The results of Callison's strategic effort to find new ways of extracting revenue out of the same space resulted in the creation of a variety of new work environments. Traditional private offices, conference rooms and training rooms combine with new spaces for collaborative work, including walk-up, plug-in counters and smaller meeting rooms, team-oriented strategy rooms, and "village greens," open lounges for social interaction and data connectivity. Who needs garages?

Above: Walk-up, plug-in counters, New York.

Right: Village Green, Portland.

Below right: Private office area, Portland.

Opposite: Informal/formal meeting area, Waltham Woods.

Photography: Chris Eden.

CBT/Childs Bertman Tseckares Inc.   Palmer & Dodge LLP
Boston, Massachusetts

Leaving the dignified stone canyons of Boston's Financial District for elegant Back Bay is not a step Bostonians take lightly. For Palmer & Dodge LLP, Boston's first preeminent law firm to make such a move, relocation has dovetailed with a rethinking of the workplace for its 190-plus lawyers and 200-plus support staff. Indeed, the new, 187,000-square foot, eight-story facility, designed by CBT/Childs Bertman Tseckares, exchanges a static traditional milieu for a dynamic contemporary one. The design exploits its small, 23,000-scquare foot floors

with stepped corners by introducing a planning module for interchangeable private offices and case rooms, furnishings standards based on furniture system components, multi-purpose, high-tech conference rooms for meetings and events, a dedicated support floor with dining room, computer room and storage, and a dramatic, two-story reception area even proper Bostonians can admire.

Top left: Administrative work stations.

Top right: Typical practice floor reception.

Above left: Dining room.

Above right: Conference room.

Opposite: Two-story reception area.

Photography: Edward Jacoby.

CBT/Childs Bertman Tseckares Inc. Foley Hoag LLP
Boston, Massachusetts

Left: Coffee bar along "main street."

Below: Conference room.

Bottom: Dining room.

Opposite: Reception.

Photography: Anton Grassl.

The founders of Foley Hoag LLP, Henry Foley and Garrett Hoag, would be pleased at the fitness of the enterprise they began in 1943 as a "different kind of law firm." Its vitality is evident throughout the new, 220,000-square foot, seven-story office, designed by CBT/Childs Bertman Tseckares for 475 employees in World Trade Center West, the first office complex in Boston's newly developed Seaport District. Foley Hoag's distinctive and appealing workplace of private offices and conference rooms, which openly acknowledges the maritime neighborhood as a source of inspiration, is supported by "main street" corridors where the hard-working staff can find refuge in lounges, coffee bars, reading room, billiard room, fitness area and club room, appointed in citrus hues. Even the firm's logo, a spinning gyroscope, lends its charm as a motif in custom carpet, metal panels in stairwells, egg-shaped conference rooms and a dining facility aptly named the Gyro Cafe.

CBT/Childs Bertman Tseckares Inc. Centre Reinsurance
Hamilton, Bermuda

Your people travel often. They like teamwork, communication and interaction. And they want a work environment that is functional, flexible and ready for a casual meeting over lunch or a formal evening of business entertainment. The Hamilton, Bermuda office of Centre Reinsurance, a wholly-owned subsidiary of the Zurich Financial Services Group, gave this design brief to CBT/Childs Bertman Tseckares to develop its new, 42,000-square foot, three-story facility. What makes the outcome so provocative is the aura of efficiency, elegance and wit surrounding private offices, open-plan work stations, meeting areas and conference center. The appearance is more than skin deep. The sophisticated conference center sees regular use by related organizations, unique building materials are holding up well, and sophisticated building systems are successfully conserving energy, water and other natural resources so scarce and costly to Bermuda.

Above: Boardroom in conference center.

Far left: Interior staircase.

Left: Conference center cafe.

Photography: Edward Jacoby.

CBT/Childs Bertman Tseckares Inc.　Boston Stock Exchange
Boston, Massachusetts

Above: Entrance to visitors' gallery.

Right: Central trading area.

Below: Boardroom.

Photography: Edward Jacoby.

Bigger seems better in today's economy. Yet size hasn't deterred the Boston Stock Exchange. A vigorous and growing BSE, founded in 1834 as the third U.S. stock exchange, makes sense for Boston, the third largest investment management center in the world, eclipsed only by New York and London. When CBT/Childs Bertman Tseckares relocated the BSE to its new, 40,000-square foot home, the challenge was to retrofit a 19th century building with trading positions for expanding 21st-century operations. The outcome combines looks and brains. Sustaining the striking central trading area, data wall, visitors' gallery and broadcast facilities is a massive infrastructure robust enough to keep pace with the fastest growing stock exchange in America.

CMSS Architects, P.C.

Cotton, Incorporated
Cary, North Carolina

In the mid-1960s, American consumers fell in love with double-knit polyester and other textiles woven in new "easy-care" synthetic fibers. In response, domestic cotton growers established a research and promotion program to celebrate the virtues of cotton. It was a defining moment for American apparel and agriculture with the creation of Cotton, Incorporated as an independent, non-profit entity. The ultimate result was the restoration of cotton as a premium fiber. With this proud legacy in mind, Cotton, Incorporated asked CMSS Architects to design its new world headquarters, laboratory and light manufacturing facility in Cary, North Carolina. The goal was to consolidate scattered activi- ties into a 21st-century facility. Major design challenges were to project a corporate image while maximizing research space and providing an educational experience for visitors. The result is two new buildings: a formal, 36,600 square foot corporate headquarters joined by a pedestrian bridge to an 88,400 square foot, high-tech laboratory. A circulation pattern was established to separate the researchers from the guests, while allowing visitors to observe cotton research. Floor to ceiling glass walls provide a window for the guests into the laboratory areas. The attractiveness, comfort and versatility of the new facility mirror the properties that have made cotton the fabric of our lives.

Above left: Monumental stairway in lobby.

Above right: Textiles laboratory.

Right: Pedestrian bridge leading to laboratory building.

Far right: Executive conference room.

Opposite: Two story lobby rotunda.

Photography: Judy Davis/ Hoachlander Davis Photography.

CMSS Architects, P.C.

CentreGreen One
Cary, North Carolina

When businesses come to Raleigh, capital of North Carolina, and the largest city in the legendary Research Triangle, chances are they will lease commercial office space in properties such as the recently completed CentreGreen One. This upscale, 101,775 square foot, three-story corporate office building located in Cary, part of the greater Raleigh area, was designed by CMSS Architects for Highwoods Properties. CentreGreen One is the first phase of a five-building campus that will surround a central park. One of the key goals for the public space in CentreGreen One was to appeal to both conservative and high-tech enterprises. According to Highwoods Properties, one of the nation's largest commercial real estate companies, the finely crafted, two-story lobby of glass walls, hardwood trim, barrel vaulted ceilings and marble floors has achieved this objective with distinction.

Above left: Lobby waiting alcove.

Above right: Masonry and woodworking details.

Below: View towards elevators.

Opposite: Balcony.

Photography: Judy Davis/Hoachlander Davis Photography.

CMSS Architects, P.C.

iXL Regional Headquarters
Richmond, Virginia

Reorganization has been the reality of the Internet-driven economy faced by numerous young enterprises and the architects who serve them. iXL Enterprises was a global consulting firm that helped companies use the power of emerging technologies and advanced business strategies to build stronger, more profitable relationships with their customers, employees, and business partners. CMSS Architects designed iXL's new 60,000 square foot, three-story regional headquarters for 300 employees in Richmond, Virginia, to facilitate just this kind of reorganization. Since iXL had recently merged with another high-tech company, it wanted the facility to help establish a new regional identity, create an environment to cultivate pride and vitality in employees, engage customers, and encourage ongoing employee interaction. The design developed for the offices, conference rooms, computer facility, high-tech presentation room, community room, bar, and break rooms is fascinating for its skillful blending of diverse elements to produce a unique and versatile composition. Among the notable concepts used in the

Above: Lobby.

Right: Sea conference room with 700-gallon aquarium.

Opposite, above: Executive reception area.

Opposite, below: Mountain conference room with climbing wall.

Photography: Judy Davis/Hoachlander Davis Photography.

Left: Community room and bar.
Below: Client server room.

award-winning interiors were: a color scheme employing one corporate color from each company, a tactile and visual milieu of varied natural and man-made materials such as bamboo, glass, Venetian plaster and stainless steel, dramatic lighting, curvilinear design elements to contrast with the building grid, a minimal number of space standards for simplified floor reconfiguration, highly mobile, contemporary furniture, and circular internal stairs connecting the second and third floors. Since whimsically themed conference rooms were an iXL corporate standard, CMSS Architects introduced fresh ideas based on regions of the world.

These highly popular spaces have individualized features alluding to mountain, desert, polar ice cap and the sea. The quality of the office was a source of considerable pride to iXL personnel and the vibrancy of the facility defined its corporate image with dramatic style.

Conant Architects

50 East 42nd Street
Suite 2400
New York, Ny 10017
646.865.1200
646.865.1377 (Fax)
www.conantarchitects.com

Conant Architects

Boyce Products, Ltd.
New York, New York

Right: Furniture vignette.

Below: Movable partitions aligned end-to-end.

Opposite: Showroom configured as three vignette areas.

Photography: Andrea Brizzi.

Visitors to the newly completed New York showroom of Boyce Products, a Pennsylvania-based manufacturer of quality wood office furniture founded in 1983, are delighted with the open, sunny environment, coming at the end of a long corridor. It's by design, of course. The 4,000-square foot facility can be easily assembled into one large display or subdivided into three vignettes because Conant Architects has shrewdly incorporated three of Boyce's modular movable partitions, which complement the company's desks, work stations and tables. The design maximizes drama at minimal cost, using a wall of windows as back lighting for the partitions opposite a Tuscan yellow wall, a sun shade as a ceiling scrim beneath exposed ductwork, and laminated glass as elegant custom flooring to bestow an irresistible aura to the showroom and its merchandise.

Conant Architects

Heller Ehrman White & McAuliffe LLP
New York, New York

Place 85 attorneys and their support staff on five small floors totaling 50,000 square feet in New York with a short lease term and a tight budget as additional constraints, and you can appreciate what Conant Architects has accomplished with its highly functional yet aesthetically powerful office for Heller Ehrman White & McAuliffe. Good planning and inspired design have made this striking environment possible for the international law firm, which employs more than

625 attorneys and professionals in 12 offices worldwide. For example, all building materials are standard, glass is applied liberally in wall glazing, table tops and as a reception desk transition surface, and intense color and variations in lighting intensity are selectively used for visual impact and illuminating an art collection. Consequently, the impression that both employees and clients have of the private offices, administrative areas, law library, staff training facility, lunch room and

central office services facility, all laid out on floors with very little interior core space, is that of an innovative and energetic law firm—a description that could describe the architect as well.

Left: Seating in reception.

Above: Reception desk with hidden flat screen monitors.

Opposite bottom: Conference room.

Photography: David Anderson.

76

Conant Architects

T-Mobile
Parsippany, New Jersey

In the rough-and-tumble telecommunications world, T-Mobile USA (formerly VoiceStream Wireless) is emerging as one of the fastest growing nationwide wireless service providers, offering all-digital voice, messaging and high-speed wireless data services to nearly 10 million customers. Growth comes with its own consequences, of course. One has been the need to expand T-Mobile operations in three separate locations by consolidating them in one larger facility—an existing, 105,000 square foot, three-story office building in Parsippany, New Jersey, to be exact—which Conant Architects recently transformed into an effective, code-compliant, state-of-the-art workplace for 500 employees. Following a comprehensive evaluation of the 1980 structure's given condition and potential for remodeling, Conant upgraded mechanical and electrical systems, increased parking, re-oriented access for single-tenant occupancy, and establishing a corporate identity. The outcome is impressive both for its command of technology, satisfying such critical demands as a 5,000-square foot Network Operation Center, a 4,000-square foot Data Center and a "Situation Room" for emergencies, and for its attention to employees, introducing such amenities as comfortable open-

office areas, a brightly illuminated central atrium, flexible classrooms, an inviting lunchroom and a commissioned art program for which photographer Bruce Beyer portrayed the role of cellular phones in people's lives. Neville R. Ray, T-Mobile's vice president for Network & Operations, Northeast, recently complimented the new facility by noting, "The positive feedback from employees, both local and visiting, as well as clients, has helped determine that this project become a benchmark for design standards for other T-Mobile locations."

Above: Team configuration of work stations.

Right: Coffee bar.

DMJM Rottet

515 South Flower Street
Los Angeles, CA 90071
213.593.8300
213.593.8610 (Fax)
info@dmjmrottet.com

DMJM Rottet

BMC Software, Inc., a leader in enterprise management software, was launched in one of its founders' homes in 1980. Two decades later, the company maintains offices worldwide, has revenues (2002) of some $1.3 billion, and occupies a new, one million-square foot headquarters in Houston, with interiors designed by DMJM Rottet and building architecture by DMJM Design. Yet the phased development of BMC's Houston headquarters maintains the company's entrepreneurial drive with an innovative campus of striking glass and concrete buildings. Though the interiors shelter BMC from Houston's hot summers, their open spaces, team areas and spare, elegant forms keep employees very much at home—in touch with the landscape and each other.

Left: Visitor center lobby.

Above: Marketing department prefunction.

Below left: Employee fitness.

Below right: Training room.

Opposite: Break room in general office space.

Photography: Nick Merrick/ Hedrich Belssing.

DMJM Rottet

Paul, Hastings, Janofsky & Walker, LLP
Los Angeles, California

Think of a law office flooded with natural light and views—an uncommon sight for a profession that fiercely guards its privacy—and you have grasped the innovative concept behind the new, 190,000-square foot Los Angeles headquarters of Paul, Hastings, Janofsky & Walker, designed by DMJM Rottet. The international law firm has provided clients with timely, professional service and superior legal counsel since its founding by a young group of Harvard Law School graduates in 1951. Its youthful outlook remains visible in the modern aesthetics, neutral palette and angled planes of the new office, highlighted by a two-story reception atrium, private offices with glass walls and clerestories, custom work stations, partners' dining hall, employee lunch room, law library and data center housing 500 employees of a firm ranked 22nd in the nation in American Lawyer's gross revenues survey for 2002.

Right: Private office.

Below left: Conference room.

Below right: Administrative work stations.

Bottom right: Perimeter corridor.

Opposite: Two-story reception atrium.

Photography: Nick Merrick/ Hedrich Belssing.

DMJM Rottet

DMJM Design
Los Angeles, California

Left: Corridor to conference rooms.

Below left: Typical work stations.

Below right: Reception looking toward DMJM Rottet's studio.

Opposite: Conference room.

Photography: Nick Merrick/ Hedrich Belssing.

It's fascinating to see what a design firm designs for itself, and the new, 125,000-square foot Los Angeles headquarters of DMJM, one of the world's leading architecture and engineering firms, designed by DMJM Rottet, doesn't disappoint. Located downtown in the ARCO Plaza complex, the facility supports DMJM's commitment to the design studio environment by establishing an open office throughout the professional services studios. As a result, even principals and senior executives occupy open work stations in a dynamic space where everyone is encouraged to excel.

YELLOW

DMJM Rottet

DMJM Rottet
Houston, Texas

Left: Studio.

Bottom: Gallery.

Bottom right: Street-level facade.

Photography: Nick Merrick/ Hedrich Belssing.

Passersby in downtown Houston are treated to a visual delight each time they walk past the historic Neils Esperson building, where the new 6,000-square foot Houston office of DMJM Rottet recently opened at street level with a sleek, modern interior. Departing from conventional workplace schemes, the office combines a studio with gallery and showroom areas under a 14-foot high ceiling, exploiting its sidewalk exposure to display work in progress from the firm and the local artist community. The studio could easily be mistaken for an art gallery or fashion boutique. Yet there's no uncertainty about its function. As developed by principal Lauren Rottet, FAIA, DMJM Rottet's distinctive environment clearly separates new and old architectural elements, explicitly identifying what the new interiors add to the existing space, and supports egalitarianism in the workplace, so that no private offices interrupt a space offering sunlight and views for all—including Houstonians looking inside every working day.

Francis Cauffman Foley Hoffmann, Architects Ltd.

2120 Arch Street
Philadelphia, PA 19103
215.568.8250
215.568.2639 (Fax)
www.fcfh-did.com

Francis Cauffman Foley Hoffmann, Architects Ltd.

Young Conaway Stargatt & Taylor, LLP
Wilmington, Delaware

From its founding in 1959 as a litigation-oriented practice, Young Conaway Stargatt & Taylor, LLP has grown into one of the largest and most prestigious law firms in Delaware, with over 80 attorneys and over 30 legal assistants in two offices active in all areas of civil practice. Steady growth recently prompted the firm to seek more than space, how-

ever. Working with Francis Cauffman Foley Hoffmann, Architects, the attorneys rethought the culture of their firm so that their new, 85,000-square-foot, four-story, contemporary Wilmington office is as versatile and efficient as those of New York and Washington competitors. Modular perimeter offices easily convert from two partners to three associ-

ates, the conference center offers advanced meeting facilities, central reception simplifies access control, and all support functions are centralized in the core of this dynamic environment.

Above: Conference center.

Right: Perimeter and interior offices.

Opposite, left: Central reception.

Photography: Don Pearse.

Francis Cauffman Foley Hoffmann, Architects Ltd.

Merck & Co., U.S. Human Health Division
Training & Professional Development Center café
Lansdale, Pennsylvania

Left: Servery.

Top: Main dining room.

Above: Seminar dining room.

Photography: Don Pearse.

Although daylight is unavailable in the Lansdale, Pennsylvania warehouse where the U.S. Human Health Division of pharmaceutical giant Merck & Co. operates its new, 17,000-square-foot dining facility in the Training & Professional Development Center, it's not missed. The Center, designed by Francis Cauffman Foley Hoffmann, Architects, serves 250 lunches daily in public, semi-private and private dining rooms. Just don't call it a cafeteria. Equipped for training, presentation and after-hours study as well as dining, the facility boasts modern building systems, advanced audiovisual equipment, plus lighting and interiors that create a restaurant-style ambiance. Bon appetit!

Francis Cauffman Foley Hoffmann, Architects Ltd.

Bristol-Myers Squibb
Dining/Servery Facility Upgrade
New Brunswick, New Jersey

Left: Cyber Cafe.
Below: Servery.
Photography: Don Pearse.

With a change from manufacturing to research and development at the New Brunswick, New Jersey campus of Bristol-Myers Squibb, the global producer and distributor of pharmaceuticals, retained Francis Cauffman Foley Hoffmann, Architects to transform the existing, 16,000-square-foot dining facility into a multi-functional space. The centrally located cafeteria now provides a warm, inviting place for informal gatherings where employees and visitors can convene near the main campus entrance, as well as a new "plug and play" Cyber Cafe for business meetings. Though the facility can host management presentations to all employees on site, mobile planters and multilevel ceiling soffits scale it down for everyday use.

Francis Cauffman Foley Hoffmann, Architects Ltd.

The Heart Hospital at Geisinger Wyoming Valley
Wilkes Barre, Pennsylvania

The Heart Hospital at Geisinger Medical Center in Wilkes-Barre, Pennsylvania is Geisinger Health System's newest means to serving over two million people in 31 counties. Geisinger, a respected health care provider founded in 1915, has incorporated a large, inpatient/outpatient cardiology and cardiothoracic surgery center for excellence in the new 50,000-square-foot, three-story facility. The Heart Hospital features state-of-the-art invasive and non-invasive procedure labs, recovery beds, a physician clinic, and both an outpatient diagnostic center and an outpatient cardiovascular fitness center. A fresh, modern interior design incorporating warm, natural materials with the spectacular views of the valley below creates a calm, healing environment for the community it serves. Geisinger CEO Glenn Steel, Jr., comments, "This is the best facility I've ever seen."

Right: Waiting room.

Below: Cardiovascular fitness center.

Photography: Don Pearse.

Francis Cauffman Foley Hoffmann, Architects Ltd.

Morgan, Lewis & Bockius, LLP
Conference Center Expansion and Vertical Expansion
Philadelphia, Pennsylvania

One of the 10 largest law firms in the United States with more than 1,000 lawyers in 13 offices worldwide, Morgan, Lewis & Bockius, founded in Philadelphia in 1873, has always balanced respect for legal tradition with modern administration. Its recent 50,000-square-foot conference center expansion and vertical expansion for some 300 attorneys and support staff in its Philadelphia office, designed by Francis Cauffman Foley Hoffmann, Architects, exemplifies its outlook by creating a flexible, multi-functional environment to address the firm's need for a conference area combining privacy for meetings with openness for large business functions. The gracious, new, transitional-style space features pivoting doors that open for large gatherings and natural light, and close for private conference rooms. The latest in communications technology is available—discreetly housed within the millwork, of course.

Above left: Conference center reception.

Top: Lounge.

Above: Elevator lobby.

Photography: Don Pearse.

96

Gary Lee Partners

360 West Superior Street
Chicago, IL 60610
312.640.8300
312.640.8301 (Fax)
www.garyleepartners.com

Gary Lee Partners

Gary Lee Partners

Madison Dearborn Partners
London, England

Above, directly: Interior conference room.

Above, center: Managing director's office.

Above, top: Office corridor and offices.

Photography: Mario Carrieri/Carrieri Photography.

Madison Dearborn Partners, a Chicago-based private equity investment firm, located its first European office in London's Mayfair District. The 500-square meter (5,380-square feet) facility, housing 15 professionals was designed and constructed within a compressed, eight-month schedule. The London office offers a collegial environment with advanced technology, flexible infrastructure within an effective layout. Great care was taken in designing this office to incorporate the design vocabulary established by Gary Lee Partners for their Chicago office, while still respecting the unique culture of this geographic location. The location of private offices on the perimeter provides access to city views while the placement of the support functions within the building core maximizes space utilization in an unusual building floor plate. Complimenting the design features a demountable wall system with a wall-mounted furniture system will aid in future reconfigurations. Standard office designs promote contents only —"briefcase moves" as clerestory panels between offices allow natural light to filter into the core areas. Large, glass pivot-doors utilized in the lobby elevation expand their distinctively visible building presence.

Above: Office entry doors from tenant lobby to reception.

Left: Reception desk and seating.

Gary Lee Partners

Winston & Strawn
Los Angeles, California

The visual concepts "light", "crisp", and "clean" characterize the design intent established for Winston & Strawn's 50,000-square foot Los Angeles office. The Chicago-based law firm, Winston & Strawn, founded in 1853, is one of the nation's oldest and most prestigious firms with 60 attorneys in Los Angeles and more that 850 attorneys worldwide. The firm's goal, to establish a Los Angeles presence that reflects contemporary West Coast culture while respecting the traditional values of its Chicago-based headquarters, has been achieved in their space by simple geometric forms, a light color-palette, and an abundance of natural light with exterior views. The refined details, of marble, glass and steel, found in the sculptural staircase, exemplify the quality and affirm the legacy of the firm.

Above: Main conference room.

Below left: Reception.

Below right: Corridor with attorneys' offices.

Opposite: Internal stair.

Photography: Steve Hall/Hedrich Blessing.

Gary Lee Partners

Latham & Watkins
Chicago, Illinois

The spectacular views from the Sears Tower provide an inspirational backdrop for Latham & Watkins' 175-attorney office in Chicago. Gary Lee Partners was commissioned by the international law firm to renovate its existing twenty year-old space and accommodate expansion to occupy more the 106,000 square feet. The construction of a 24-hour, independent conference center was the first phase of the renovation. The design was influenced by the architecture and visual rhythm of the Sears Tower's exterior and established the vocabulary that was later applied to the remaining 100,000-square feet of office space. The Conference Center is composed of re-configurable rooms and furniture, ample wiring capacity via raised floors, state-of-the-art audio-visual equipment, a catering kitchen, administrative service center, breakout areas, private lounge, and club/residential style furnishing that provide comfort during extend stay functions. The firm remained fully operational during the entire renovation, which occurred

Right: Conference room.

Below: Main conference room seen from reception.

Opposite, upper left: Conference center entrance.

Opposite, lower left: Typical attorney floor.

Photography: Steve Hall/Hedrich Blessing.

in six-phases over a two
and a half year period. In the
office renovation some existing details were salvaged
and incorporated with new
furnishings, carpet, finishes,
millwork, demountable wall
systems, and updated technology to create an elegant,
effective space.

Above: Library.

Right: Attorney's office.

Gerner Kronick + Valcarcel, Architects, PC

443 Park Avenue South
2nd Floor
New York, NY 10017
212.679.6362
212.679.5877
www.gkvarchitects.com

Gerner Kronick + Valcarcel, Architects, PC

Gerner Kronick + Valcarcel, Architects, PC

Clear Channel Entertainment
New York, New York

Top right: Media presentation theater.

Above left: Internal stair.

Above right: Open plan area.
Left: Reception.

Opposite: Seating group in reception.

Photography: Paul Warchol.

Like the Wizard of Oz behind his curtain, much of the entertainment world remains invisible to the audience. That's why one of the world's leading promoters and marketers of live entertainment can restore an historic property, as Clear Channel Entertainment has recently done with the services of Gerner Kronick + Valcarcel, Architects, before locating the employees at the terra-cotta-clad Candler Building, a 220,000-square foot, 24-story, early 20th century skyscraper in midtown Manhattan. The attractive new executive offices, boardroom, executive dining, media presentation theater, conference room, cafeteria and ground floor lobby are backed by upgraded mechanical and electrical systems, new elevators and new finishes and interior furnishings. Happily, fans of such entertainers and organizations as Backstreet Boys, Madonna and Supercross and Monster Trucks won't have a clue.

Gerner Kronick + Valcarcel, Architects, PC

HypoVereinsbank
New York, New York

Crisp, modern and efficient, the new, 130,000-square foot, five-level U.S. headquarters for HypoVereinsbank in New York, designed by Gerner Kronick + Valcarcel, Architects, reflects the bank and its parent, HVB Group, Germany's second largest private-sector bank, with over 66,500 employees, 2,100 branch offices, total assets of approximately EUR 712 billion and over 8.5 million customers. The new office values practicality by assigning almost everyone to open-plan work stations rather than private offices. Yet pragmatism does not preclude the privacy of small huddle rooms and larger conference rooms, which are vital to a facility that includes executive and general offices, boardroom, trading floor, teller services, computer center and lunchroom, all tracing a precise planning grid.

Top right: Conference room.

Upper left: Executive reception area.

Upper right: Executive offices.

Left: Huddle room.

Opposite: Internal stair.

Photography: Paul Warchol.

Gerner Kronick + Valcarcel, Architects, PC

MTV Network Ad Sales
New York, New York

"I want my MTV!" From 377.3 million households spanning 166 countries and territories comes this adolescent chorus, confirming the drawing power of Music Television or MTV, Nickelodeon, VH1, The New TNN, and other cable television programs from MTV Networks, part of media giant Viacom. Media buyers visiting 84,000-square foot MTV Network Ad Sales in New York, designed by Gerner Kronick + Valcarcel, Architects, don't expect to see conventional accommodations for the reception, executive and general offices, conference rooms, pantries and other facilities, and they're not disappointed.

Above: Video wall.

Right: Reception seating.

Far right: Reception desk.

Below right: Conference room.

Below far right: General office area.

Photography: David Joseph.

Gerner Kronick + Valcarcel, Architects, PC

Adobe Training Center
New York, New York

You won't forget your visit to the briefing and communications center, a cluster of conference rooms, office space and a teleconference facility, at Adobe's new, 15,000-square foot Training Center in Manhattan, designed by Gerner Kronick + Valcarcel, Architects. After all, software products from Adobe, one of the world's largest PC software companies (annual revenues exceed $1.2 billion), enable customers to create, manage and deliver visually rich content. Adobe's desire to surround customers with a comparable physical environment resulted in the striking new space, which features a nautilus-shaped "wooden brick" wall, colored glass walls, and sophisticated computer technology and architecture, seamlessly integrated.

Right: Reception seating.

Lower right: Teleconference facility.

Below: Reception desk.

Photography: Mark Ross.

Gerner Kronick + Valcarcel, Architects, PC

Sillerman Company
New York, New York

Above left: Reception.
Above right: Conference room.
Right: Executive offices.
Photography: Paul Warchol.

An innovative and dynamic environment seemed right for Sillerman Company, a thriving holding company for sports, entertainment and talent businesses at the time it retained Gerner Kronick + Valcarcel, Architects to create a 25,000-square foot, two-story New York office. Indeed, visiting the lively, contemporary facility, which included executive offices, conference rooms, lunch room, gym and restrooms, was like stepping on stage.

Griswold, Heckel & Kelly Associates, Inc.
and Space/Management Programs

GHK
55 West Wacker Drive
6th Floor
Chicago, IL 60601

Space/Management Programs
55 West Wacker Drive
6th Floor
Chicago, IL 60601

312.263.6605
312.263.1228 (Fax)
www.ghk.net

New York
Boston
Baltimore
Washington, DC

Griswold, Heckel & Kelly Associates, Inc. and Space/Management Programs

Ernst & Young LLP
Shared Services Location
Indianapolis, Indiana

Right: Relaxation room.

Below left: Workstations with putting green.
Below right: Entrance with 750-gallon aquarium.

Bottom right: Media/lunch-room.

Opposite: Office corridor.

Photography: Charlie Mayer.

Let people facing long working shifts imagine "where people love to come to work" and what happens? For Ernst & Young LLP, the U.S. arm of Ernst & Young International, Ltd., with 30,000 employees in 85 cities, the answer could be its innovative, new, 50,000-square foot Shared Services facility in Indianapolis, Indiana, designed by GHK for over 300 personnel. The first of several such facilities, Shared Services acknowledges employees' needs by blending standard and non-traditional work environments in its training facilities, support space, media/lunchroom, game room, putting green and relaxation rooms—all framed by multiple ceiling planes, canted walls and theatrical lighting—plus outdoor recreational opportunities. Those long working shifts may seem shorter now.

Griswold, Heckel & Kelly Associates, Inc. and Space/Management Programs

Rooms with views are treasured in New York's canyons. Like other city residents, Bain & Company—one of the world's most prestigious strategy consulting firms with over 2,800 employees serving clients through 26 offices in 20 countries—is showcasing dramatic vistas from the 24th and 25th floors of the recently completed Reuter's Building in Times Square to inspire employees and clients in its first New York office, a 35,000-square foot facility designed by GHK for 105 employees. The elegant setting provides views

and natural light in all of its teamwork-oriented "neighborhood" environments, which GHK delineates with such hard-walled elements as conference rooms, library, copy/pantry areas and private offices partitioned by interior walls of clear and textured glass, as well as clusters of open-plan work stations standardized on 42-inch high panels. While the design culminates in the sweeping reception and client contact areas, where the main conference room opens to accommodate large informal meetings or formal

cocktail parties, even a room as humble as the main pantry sports a magnificent view of the Empire State Building.

Top: Main pantry.

Above: Executive breakout room.

Below left: Main conference room.

Opposite: Reception seen from elevator lobby.

Photography: Peter Paige.

Griswold, Heckel & Kelly Associates, Inc. and Space/Management Programs

Quaker Food & Beverages Headquarters Chicago, Illinois

Call it a second helping if you wish, but Quaker Oats was so pleased with GHK's design for its headquarters in the 1990s that it asked the design firm to create optimum space use strategies and a design for its relocated headquarters in the 21st century. The Chicago-based food and beverage processor, noted for Gatorade, Rice-A-Roni, Pasta-Roni, Near East side dishes and Aunt Jemima mixes and syrups as well as its signature oats, was acquired by Pepsico in 2001. In developing Quaker's new, 450,000-square foot headquarters for 1,200 employees, GHK introduced a scheme based on a spinning top, characterized by curvilinear forms that promote movement and impromptu collaboration, modularity and flexibility to let a single office or pod of work stations occupy the same footprint, and "interactive zones" off elevator lobbies offering a range of conference rooms and beverage cafes to support teamwork. Third helping, anyone?

Top right: General office space.
Above: Typical floor entry.
Left: Executive reception.
Above left: Private office.
Opposite: Interactive zone.
Photography: Charlie Mayer.

Griswold, Heckel & Kelly Associates, Inc. and Space/Management Programs

Vocus, Inc.
Lanham, Maryland

Above right: Public entrance.

Above left: Open task area beside entertainment area.

Left: Reception.

Below left: Core fitness area.

Photography: Michael Dersin.

Why would a technology company like Vocus, the leading provider of Web-based software for public relations automation, house its operations in a "flex" building, particularly a single-story, suburban commercial structure in Lanham, Maryland featuring high ceilings and little else—not even mechanical, electrical or plumbing systems? Vocus, working closely with GHK, was able to outfit the empty shell with exactly the building systems it needed, along with whimsical yet cost-effective interiors for a new, 23,000-square foot, 140-person corporate office. Its requirement for flexible space, uniquely suited for alleviating work-related stress, is supported by a concentric floor plan featuring a central core fitness area for de-stressing, a conferencing area, an open task area and an entertainment area, enlivened through a layering of playful geometric shapes and colors and industrial accent materials. Indeed, the office's vitality could give "flex" buildings a good name.

Gwathmey Siegel & Associates Architects

475 Tenth Avenue
New York, NY 10018
212.947.1240
212.967.0890 (Fax)
www.gwathmeysiegel.com

Gwathmey Siegel & Associates Architects

Gwathmey Siegel & Associates Architects

Morgan Stanley Dean Witter & Co.
World Headquarters
New York, New York

Morgan Stanley Dean Witter & Co., one of the world's leading investment banks, is on the move again. Having relocated in the 1990s from its historic Wall Street headquarters to a striking, new, 52-story midtown Manhattan skyscraper, designed by Gwathmey Siegel & Associates Architects, it has made a significant investment in its facilities by remodeling its 20,000-square foot lobby and developing a new, 20,000-square foot, subterranean cafeteria, both designed by Gwathmey Siegel. The public lobby, a majestic expanse of granite, marble, wood, carpet and stainless steel, takes employees directly to escalators, stairs and an access bridge that descend to a full-service, 500-seat cafeteria, kitchen and servery, where employees can have meals, coffee, lunch to go, or meetings that can accommodate the entire work force. Judging from their high volume of use, the new facilities are paying steady dividends.

Above left: Cafeteria tray return, escalators and stairs.

Above right: Cafeteria servery.

Left: Lobby.

Opposite: Lobby access to cafeteria.

Photography: Peter Aaron and Jeff Goldberg/Esto Photographics.

Gwathmey Siegel & Associates Architects

PepsiCo
World Headquarters Master Plan &
Facilities Upgrade
Purchase, New York

Legendary buildings can evolve gracefully, as PepsiCo's headquarters in Purchase, New York recently demonstrated with an impressive upgrade by Gwathmey Siegel & Associates Architects. This seven-building complex, originally designed by Edward Durrell Stone on a 144-acre site for the global purveyor of convenient foods and beverages, is legendary for its gardens of sculpture by masters such as Auguste Rodin, Alexander Calder and Alberto Giacometti. Having revised PepsiCo's master plan in 1993, Gwathmey

Above left: Renovated dining room with view towards addition.

Above right: Lounge in Leadership Conference Center.

Left: Breakout rooms.

Opposite: Leadership Conference Center.

Photography: Paul Warchol.

Siegel has now created new 400-seat Cafeteria and Dining Facilities, 150-seat Leadership Conference Center and Gallery and Dining Room Addition, encompassing some 52,500 square feet. What makes the design so compelling is that it combines respect for the original architecture with a new vision of modern design serving contemporary business and state-of-the-art technology. From the hardwood, marble, and stainless steel-lined Dining Room, overlooking Pepsico's serene gardens, to the wood, carpet and reinforced fiberglass-lined Leadership Conference Center, where superb acoustics make microphones optional, PepsiCo can effectively market such brands as Pepsi, Fritos, Tropicana and Gatorade to a waiting world.

Gwathmey Siegel
& Associates Architects

Ronald S. Lauder Foundation
New York, New York

If a client compliments his architect through multiple assignments, the new, 6,000-square foot Manhattan office for the Ronald S. Lauder Foundation, designed by Gwathmey Siegel & Associates Architects, honors both parties alike. Gwathmey Siegel had designed Ronald Lauder's business office six years earlier. Since Lauder wanted the new space to establish a fresh image for 30 employees of the Foundation, which is devoted to rebuilding Jewish life in Europe, the architect created a unique environment of barrel-vaulted, stainless steel ceilings, cherry millwork, textured glass, rubber flooring, carpet and selections from Lauder's renowned Secessionist art and furniture collection. Amidst corridors doubling as art galleries, Foundation workers love their workplace.

Above: Conference room.

Left: Administrative work station.

Far left: Private office.

Opposite: Corridor.

Photography: Michael Moran.

Gwathmey Siegel
& Associates Architects

D'Arcy Masius Benton & Bowles, Inc.
World Headquarters
New York, New York

You won't find theatergoers admiring one of the most dramatic spaces in Manhattan's fabled theater district—the 8,000-square foot, two-story volume at the heart of the 300,000-square foot, 14-story world headquarters for D'Arcy Masius Benton & Bowles, designed by Gwathmey Siegel & Associates Architects. Removing a floor in the skyscraper housing the respected advertising agency exposed a structure of diagonal supporting trusses and created a memorable yet functional presentation/conference complex of conference rooms that visitors enter via a stainless steel and slate stairway. It's just one of numerous appropriate design flourishes for the ad shop that made Coca-Cola a household name back in 1906.

Above: Presentation/conference area stairway.

Right: Cantilevered conference room facade.

Photography: Paul Warchol.

H. Hendy Associates

2415 Campus Drive
Suite 110
Irvine, CA 92612
949.851.3080
949.851.0807 (Fax)
www.hhendy.com

H. Hendy Associates

H. Hendy Associates

Pacific Sunwear
Anaheim, California

Specialty apparel retailer Pacific Sunwear believes that although their teenage and young adult customers may never see the campus, chances are they would love the spirited, 151,000-square foot, three-story headquarters and adjoining distribution center and warehouse, designed by H. Hendy Associates. Pacific Sunwear's casual apparel, accessories and footwear for surfing, skate boarding and snowboarding, distributed through 782 stores nationwide, succeed because the retailer has listened to its customers since 1980. The same could be said of the campus. To help different brands share design and merchandising resources, the facility establishes optimum adjacencies, maximizes daylight by grouping offices along the perimeter, and provides such resources as a high-tech boardroom, flexible meeting/training rooms that convert into a 300-seat auditorium for fashion shows, mock-up retail stores, and Café Pac Sun, a bistro customers would love.

Above right: Café Pac Sun.

Top right: Boardroom with surfboard conference table.

Above left: Corridor with mock display.

Opposite: Reception.

Photography: Paul Bielenberg.

H. Hendy Associates

LeadersOnline
Aliso Viejo, California

Like any good Internet business, LeadersOnline, the Internet-enhanced recruiting subsidiary of Heidrick & Struggles International, a worldwide executive recruiting firm, for mid-level executives and professionals, wanted its new, 24,000-square foot, Aliso Viejo, California headquarters immediately. What's notable about the design by H. Hendy Associates is not just that it honored the tight schedule and restricted budget, but that it produced an excellent workplace. LeadersOnline wanted a visually open office for 100 employees that could foster teamwork and interaction in a flexible, mobile and sophisticated setting.

Thoughtful design and specifications not only achieved the recruiter's goals for time and cost, they exceeded its expectations for performance and aesthetics.

Left: Open-plan work stations.

Above left: Cafe.

Above right: General office area.

Opposite: Lobby.

Photography: Paul Bielenberg.

H. Hendy Associates   Large Automobile Manufacturer
Phoenix, Arizona

Below left: Reception and lobby area.

Right: Walkway to conference room.

Below right: Serpentine work stations.

Opposite, upper right: General office area.

Photography: Paul Bielenberg.

We all know the feeling when motorists forget where their cars are in vast parking lots. Even the Phoenix, Arizona-based financial services division of a major automobile manufacturer encountered this problem in its new and elegantly tailored, 84,745 square foot, 2-story office, designed by H. Hendy Associates. The facility's large floor plates provided great flexibility for space planning. However, they also required a wayfinding strategy. H. Hendy's solution was to use architectural elements and color to phrase visual clues to major circulation paths and common areas. Seeking inspiration inside and outside automobiles, the design incorporates such car materials as cherry wood, chrome accents and leather, and combines them with bold colors and contrasting geometric shapes that represent the rustic Arizona landscape, giving the facility its own momentum.

H. Hendy Associates

SubZero Constructors
Lake Forest, Calfornia

Left: Lobby.

Below right: Work stations.

Bottom right: Kitchen area.

Photography: Paul Bielenberg.

How sensible for SubZero Constructors, a refrigerated warehouse construction firm in Lake Forest, Calfornia, to want its 6,000-square foot headquarters to be anything but cold. In fact, SubZero's president specifically asked H. Hendy Associates to design a workplace that embodied "simplicity, harmony and balance." The space encompasses administrative offices as well as large, open-plan areas for the design of complex refrigeration systems for such clients as M&M Mars and Ralph's Supermarkets. What distinguishes the installation is its creative use of the existing high, exposed ceilings and, expressed in a design of cool colors, natural materials and clean geometric shapes. It's a convincing example of the California "industrial zen" feel that SubZero's customers must know well.

Heery International, Inc.

999 Peachtree Street
Atlanta, GA 30309
404.881.9880
404.875.1283 (Fax)
www.heery.com

Heery International, Inc.

Equant
Atlanta, Georgia

If every industry has bragging rights, Equant, which became part of France Telecom in 2001, could boast of being the leading global data and IP network services provider for thousands of multinational businesses in over 220 countries. Its attractive new, 180,000-square foot, nine-floor Atlanta office, designed by Heery International, shows further signs of leadership in introducing some 975 employees to universal floor plans that allow them to relocate without altering walls or work stations. Besides minimizing downtime, the facility, which consists of private and open offices, conference/sales marketing center, computer room and executive offices, aligns U.S. corporate standards with European standards at Equant's home office in Slough, England. Equant employees may never equate their workplace with Slough, England, but they now report to an airy, open environment with "centralized nodes" for shared activities, including cafes.

Left: Conference room.

Upper left: Lounge in conference/sales marketing center.

Upper right: Door to elevator lobby.

Opposite: Reception desk and seating.

Photography: Jonathan Hillyer.

138

Heery International, Inc.

Private Corporate Client
Atlanta, Georgia

Above: Open-plan offices.

Left: Breakout space.

Below: Conference area with garage doors.

Opposite: Coffee bar.

Photography: Jonathan Hillyer.

Want to work in a "hip" office park? To attract 30 young, talented Web-based designers to staff an Atlanta corporation's 24/7 operation, Heery International set forth to creatively transform a 9,000-square foot space in a corporate office park. Ceilings were removed, concrete floors were exposed, and such hallmarks of loft living cherished by young, high-tech workers, such as pool and ping pong tables doubling as conference tables, rubber flooring in main corridors doubling as indoor track surfaces, and garage doors doubling as retractable walls, were installed. The result: a flexible, comfortable and "hip" office.

Heery International, Inc.

Southern Polytechnic State University
School of Architecture
Marietta, Georgia

A great campus demands more than one great building. However, architecture's power to confer credibility as well as capability to colleges and universities one building at a time is being harnessed with increasing sophistication in projects like the new 80,000-square foot, four-story School of Architecture, designed by Heery International, at Southern Polytechnic State University in Marietta, Georgia. Founded in 1948, Southern Polytechnic is a residential, co-educational member of the University System of Georgia serving 4,000 students at its wooded, 232-acre campus northwest of Atlanta. Of course, the project's primary goal was to facilitate the teaching of construction technique and the making of architecture to 300 students. But realizing the structure could do considerably more, the University worked with Heery to reinforce the southern end of the campus, project a new, progressive image, and provide a large, public space for everyday use. The award-winning design of studios, classrooms, offices, jury room, galleries, systems laboratory and shops acts as a splendid demonstration project for the School.

Above: Studio.
Left: Gallery.
Below: Corridor.
Opposite: Atrium.
Photography: Michael Parker.

HOK

Amsterdam*

Atlanta   Madrid*

Berlin*   Mexico City

Brisbane   Milan*

Brussels*   New York

Chicago   Orlando

Dallas   Ottawa

Frankfurt*   Paris*

Hong Kong   San Francisco

Houston   St. Louis

Kansas City   Tampa

London   Toronto

Los Angeles   Washington, DC

                               *European Alliance Offices

HOK

AT&T Global Network Operations Center
Northern New Jersey

What does it take to run the world's largest and most sophisticated communications network? AT&T observes that, "On an average business day, it delivers more combined data, voice and Internet traffic to more locations more reliably than any other network." It's a fact. On an average day, AT&T's global network carries 675 trillion bytes (ter-abytes) of data, the equivalent of all the books in the Library of Congress every 45 minutes and more data than any other carrier in the industry, as well as 300 million voice calls. Accordingly, the new, 198,000-square foot, four-story Global Network Operations Center on the AT&T corporate campus in Northern New Jersey, designed by HOK, houses

Above left: Demonstration area for customers.

Upper left: Internet café.

Right: NOC floor and visitors' gallery.

Photography: Peter Paige.

700 employees as well as major customers inside a tour de force of technology and design. The award-winning space, which comprises offices, network operations center (NOC), galleries, conference center, client reception area, client dining room and amenity areas, is both a working NOC and an engaging showcase for customers to experience. By providing meticulously integrated design and engineering services to AT&T, HOK has created a unique working environment where employees and visitors can see space and data interact in extraordinary ways.

Above left: Interactive gallery.

Above right: Rotunda with musical instruments for international communications display.

HOK

Cisco Systems
Technology Center
Bedfont Lakes, London, United Kingdom

Avove: Downstairs into level 1.

Left: Executive Briefing Center reception.

Below left: Communication room.

Bottom: Top floor café.

Right: Glass screen with seating.

Photography: Peter Cook/View.

Visitors marvel at how such a big, complex and densely populated campus on the outskirts of London can be so lively. In fact, the new, 260,000-square foot Bedfont Lakes Technology Center in two four-story buildings and one three-story building for 1,200 employees of Cisco Systems, interiors designed by HOK, performs so well occupants call it "an inspirational 21st-century workplace." Not only do the open-plan and private offices, conference and training facilities, breakout areas, demonstration and technical laboratories, restaurant and satellite cafes, and gymnasium convincingly demonstrate that no one needs a dedicated work station, but desks should be assigned on an "as needed" basis. Openness and teamwork are encouraged even in the presence of cellular offices, conference rooms and "focus" rooms where individuals can work quietly. Among the techniques that make the Center livable are easily navigable floor plans based on atriums, private window offices, open plan areas, "touch down" areas for team gatherings, and transitional "gateway zones" between semi-public and private areas, a lively wayfinding program using saturated colors and geometric shapes, and abundant daylight and views of the surrounding landscape. This flexible wireless working environment is made possible by the use of Cisco's Technology Solutions, including IP telephony, throughout the facility. The contemporary interiors also happen to be fresh, imaginative and appealing, qualities that can be appreciated in one room or many.

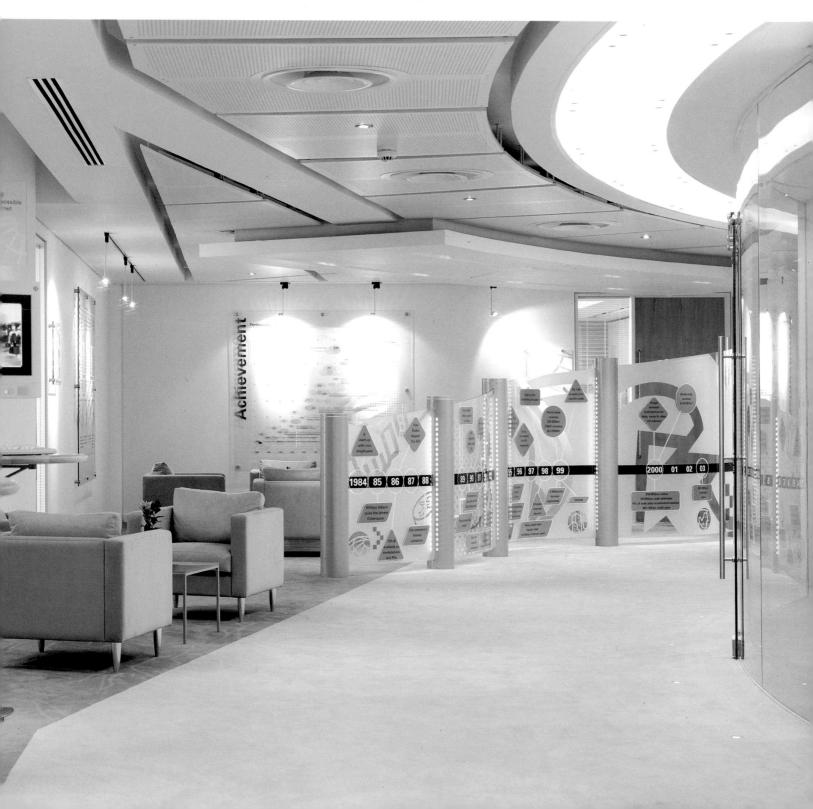

HOK

IBM e-business
Chicago, Illinois

David Ray, IBM senior real estate program manager, is candid about the edgy, new, 60,000-square foot, two-level IBM e-business office for 250 employees in Chicago, designed by HOK. "If you can't tell the instant you get out of the elevator that you are about to experience something different," he declares, "then I haven't succeeded at my job." The facility supporting IBM's Web design and hosting service eschews private offices for team environments with "shared offices," varied meeting areas, a meeting, eating and relaxing zone, and briefing center. (Briefing Center in collaboration with Design Office from Los Angeles). Definitely not your father's IBM.

Top: Reception (with Design Office).

Above left: General office area.

Above right: Breakroom/gathering zone.

Right: Presentation room (with Design Office).

Opposite: Corridor through building core.

Photography: Chris Barrett/Hedrich Blessing.

An International Investment Banking Company
Los Angeles, California

Innocent sounding, yes. But the International Investment Banking Company's request to HOK for a "classic" and "timeless" 43,000-square foot, two-level office for 159 employees in Los Angeles with clean lines and an overall tone of "understated elegance" proved immensely challenging. Ironically, the problem—integrating state-of-the-art technology with a spare modern interior of glass, stainless steel, hardwood and stone—has been subtly resolved. Thanks to careful planning and custom build outs and millwork in the private offices, open-plan work

stations, trading floor with 80 positions, conference room, training room and lunch/breakroom, advanced technology is only as visible as the Bank wishes.

Above: Serving credenza adjacent to conference/training room.

Right: Reception.

Lower left: Trading floor.

Lower right: Staff breakroom.

Photography: Hedrich Blessing.

IA Interior Architects

350 California Street
Suite 1500
San Francisco, CA 94104
415.434.3305
415.434.0330 (Fax)

www.interiorarchitects.com
k.vanert@interiorarchitects.com

Atlanta
Boston
Chicago
Costa Mesa
Dallas
Denver
London
Los Angeles

New Jersey
New York
Seattle
Shanghai
Silicon Valley
Washington, DC

IA Interior Architects

Centrica
London, United Kingdom

Making life easier for customers is the mission of London-based Centrica, providing energy, telecommunications, roadside recovery and financial services through businesses in Great Britain, Canada, the United States and Belgium. The firm set a similar goal in developing 120,000 square feet of offices for 720 employees in two buildings, both designed by Interior Architects, representing its new corporate headquarters and e-commerce businesses. As the keystone of Centrica's West London Relocation Project, the facilities feature open environments using systems furniture with low-height screens. The executive floor is appropriately furnished in limestone, zebranno wood, glass-fronted private offices, and maple wood-paneled board and executive dining rooms with vaulted ceilings. Appealing in quite a different vein are such e-commerce building amenities as a cyber cafe, restaurant, retail shop, hospitality suite, auditorium, gymnasium and hot desk room. Yet the two are hardly worlds apart: A glass corridor connects them physically and symbolically.

Above: Perimeter corridor.

Right: Open-plan area supporting window offices.

Opposite: Glass corridor between buildings.

Photography: ©Nick Hufton/View

IA Interior Architects

Pantheon Ventures
San Francisco, California

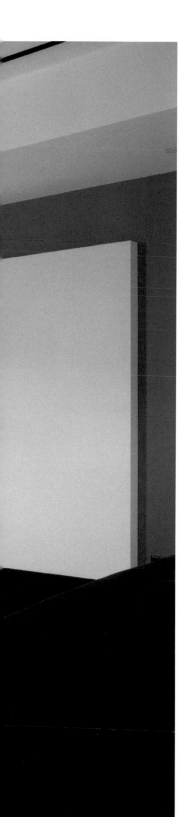

Think globally, act locally. How does Pantheon, a leading, independent, London-based provider of private equity investment products and services founded in 1982, remain disciplined and focused in serving over 480 private equity partnerships in 30 countries? When its San Francisco office needed a new, 12,000-square foot facility for 24 people, the partners asked Interior Architects for a facility reflecting Bay Area culture—in addition to providing efficient planning for future growth, offices and meeting areas with advanced technology, and a light, open space with views for all employees. From its direct view of historic Coit Tower and finishes and colors keyed to Northern California to its main conference room equipped for video conferencing on a plasma screen, the urbane San Francisco office leaves no doubt about its origins and goals.

Left: Reception.

Above: View of additional reception seating.

Top: Main conference room.

Photography: ©David Wakely

IA Interior Architects

A Financial Services Firm
New York, New York

The triumphant restoration of Lever House, an International Style landmark in midtown Manhattan designed by Skidmore, Owings & Merrill in 1950, provides an exceptional context for the sophisticated, new, 40,000-square foot, four-level office designed by David Chipperfield and Interior Architects for a Financial Services Firm. As visitors can readily perceive, the opportunity to work with a Modernist icon has been embraced with inspiration, expertise and respect. The spacious environment of private offices, open-plan work stations, meeting rooms, reception area, auditorium and 10,000-square foot trading floor for 80 traders is based on the building's original module. Beginning with the structural grid, IA layered the floor plans, carefully

Above: Reception with Sol Lewitt mural.

Below left: Trading floor.
Below right: Private office.

Opposite: Lounge with painting by Sean Scully.

Photography: ©Peter Aaron/Esto

detailed planes and simple palette of fine finishes to build an elegant, three-dimensional composition. Timeless materials such as polished marble, rich hardwoods, glass and metal have been combined with such contemporary materials as rubber flooring in a color palette of white, red and black to acknowledge the skyscraper's heritage and accommodate current and future needs, and are enriched by an evolving modern art collection. The understatement extends to the advanced technology in the trading floor and video conferencing and audio-visual systems in the auditorium, as well as new mechanical and electrical systems for the entire facility, which are discreetly installed to avoid disrupting the minimal aesthetic. Their subtlety contrasts with the boldness of artist Sol Lewitt's new mural, whose serpentine whorls fill the reception area with the energy of an uncaged boa constrictor.

Above: Elevator lobby with contemporary painting.

Right: General office view.

Kling

2301 Chestnut Street
Philadelphia, PA 19103
215.569.2900
215.569.5963 (Fax)
info@kling.us
www.kling.us

Kling

Kling

Cingular Wireless
King of Prussia, Pennsylvania

Below: Reception.

Opposite, upper left: Teaming area.

Opposite, upper right: Executive suite.

Opposite, lower right: Game room.

Photography: Tom Crane and Jeff Totaro.

Five weeks to design a 40,000-square foot regional headquarters for Cingular Wireless in King of Prussia, Pennsylvania? That's right. Timing is everything for America's second largest wireless company, which recently retained Kling to develop a reception area, executive suite, private and open offices, coffee bar, training center, conference rooms and game room for 146 employees in very short order. Cingular's goals—consolidating scattered properties and people, creating a branding statement, receiving client visitors, and supporting a quality employee base—are satisfied by a sweeping, contemporary space constituting a main corridor "spline" flanked by internal support spaces, open perimeter walls, teaming areas placed among open offices, and amenity spaces showcasing the Cingular "jack" logo and corporate culture for all to see.

Kling

Datek World Headquarters
Jersey City, New Jersey

A memorable place to witness the emergence of online brokerage has been Datek's 340,000-square foot headquarters and research facility, designed by Kling on the waterfront in Jersey City, New Jersey. This combined office, research/development data center, kitchen, servery and dining room, and walk-in education center gave 1,100 employees of the online brokerage—now part of Ameritrade, a former competitor—a flexible, efficient and ergonomic workplace that recognized its culturally distinct technological and financial components by housing them in functionally independent elements and zones. A distinctive spatial characteristic was its layering, wrapping such amenities as the lobby, cafe, pantry, copy/fax, interaction areas and supplemental telecommunications/data rooms around the base building core, and surrounding them with a systems zone of open work stations and private offices, buffered by circulation paths along the core and periphery. The scheme equipped Datek to challenge Wall Street, whose lower Manhattan bastion was visible from its windows.

Top: Conference room.

Above: Reception with view of lower Manhattan.

Lower left: Servery.

Lower right: Dining room.

Opposite: Circulation path along building core.

Photography: Tom Crane and Jeff Totaro.

164

Kling

Merrill Lynch Campus
Hopewell, New Jersey

Top left: Great room.

Above left: Conference room.

Above right: Lounge.

Below left: Dining facility.

Opposite: Meeting area in elevator lobby.

Photography: Tom Crane and Jeff Totaro.

Nothing happens overnight when you're working on the scale of Merrill Lynch's 1.8 million-square foot Hopewell Campus in central New Jersey. So how did one of the world's leading financial management and advisory companies, with offices in 37 countries and total client assets of $1.3 trillion, update its Wall Street image and reduce "Day 2 Churn" costs through a two-year, four-phase, fast-track effort? The firm retained Kling, which developed three new office and work station standards in place of six, and selected a stackable furniture system, demountable partitions and quick disconnect lighting fixtures to improve life for 6,800 employees in eight office buildings and four assembly buildings.

Kling

JPMorgan Private Client Group
Philadelphia, Pennsylvania

Whether the rich are truly "different from you and me" as F. Scott Fitzgerald asserted, they have substantial assets that they typically entrust to professional wealth managers like JPMorgan Private Client Group. To serve private banking clients in Philadelphia, JPMorgan recently retained Kling to create a new, 30,000-square foot regional office for 50 employees that would reflect the bank's historic, high-style residential setting while discreetly incorporating the latest information technology. The completed facility, tastefully appointed in 18th-century American and English style, occupies the 47th floor of prestigious One Liberty Place. Its design places client meeting areas and offices in four perimeter quadrants that enjoy panoramic views of Center City, and concentrates all service and support areas in the central core. Besides having a reception/waiting area and a series of rooms to accommodate gatherings of every size, the client meeting area opens up for entertaining with the aid of a movable wall. But of course.

Above left: Meeting room.
Above right: Open office area.
Top right: Private office.
Left: Reception/waiting area.
Photography: Tom Crane and Jeff Totaro.

The Libman Group

1180 Avenue of the Americas
Suite 1500
New York, NY 10036
212.899.5119
212.899.5120
www.libmangroup.com
info@libmangroup.com

The Libman Group

The Libman Group · Rothschild North America
New York, New York

How does a legendary house at the center of world financial markets handle rapid growth? Rothschild North America, part of the Rothschild network that provides corporate banking, investment banking, fund management, private banking and trust services, chose to remodel 100,000 square feet of office space for 250 employees on two floors, designed by The Libman Group, at 1251 Avenue of the Americas in New York's Rockefeller Center. The project began with the complete demolition and reconstruction of the 44th floor to install a state-of-the-art trading room, "grab-n-go" employee cafe, reception area and elevator lobby. It subsequently added the renovation of the executive area and corporate dining facility on the 51st floor, exploiting high ceilings and barrel-vaulted corridors to establish a new executive wing, conference center and 24/7 analyst bullpen area and virtual library. Whatever rate of growth follows, Rothschild North America seems ready to keep the pace.

Left: Employee cafe.

Below: Elevator lobby.

Opposite: Executive wing corridor.

Overleaf: Trading room.

Photography: Peter Pierce.

The Libman Group

Kana Communications
New York, New York

You can raise the caring of customers to an art by providing the information technology industry's leading external-facing CRM (customer relationship management) solutions to many of the world's largest businesses. Customers certainly come first in Kana Software's new 35,000-square foot facility for 75 employees in New York, designed by The Libman Group, which features a Client Visitation Center (CVC) for sales presentations. For example, the elevator lobby and reception area are integrated into a single, dramatic space anchored by a two-story, angled, open stair to draw visitors inside, separate access to the CVC and the main conference room buffers customers from other visitors, and the CVC's 21-seat sales conference room inspires customers with its sweeping, radial ceiling, sophisticated lighting and audio-visual equipment, private telephone/fax booths and pantry. Interestingly, in an intriguing reversal of standard practice, team-conference rooms line the perimeter, supporting an interior open-plan area, another visible reminder of Kana's distinctive outlook on business.

Left: CVC sales conference room.

Below: Main conference room.

Opposite: Reception.

Photography: Peter Pierce.

The Libman Group

Left: Parisian railroad station clock before kitchen.

Below: Living room featuring 19th-century mansion's arch.

Photography: Peter Pierce.

A former doctor's office on the ground floor of a prominent apartment building on New York City's fabled Central Park West has provided the raw material for an exquisite, 1,700-square foot private residence, designed by The Libman Group, for a corporate CEO. The apartment's distinctive appearance is achieved by combining antique furniture and architectural elements collected from old buildings with new construction, resulting in a fresh interpretation of 18th-century French classicism. Colorful details, including an arch from a 19th-century upstate New York mansion, a Parisian railroad station clock and a Laurentian ski lodge's fireplace mantel, make the hours spent here unlike any visit to the doctor.

Little Diversified Architectural Consulting

5815 Westpark Drive
Charlotte, NC 28217
704.525.6350
704.561.8700 (Fax)
www.littleonline.com

Little Diversified Architectural Consulting

Little Diversified Architectural Consulting

Steedman Wilson
Charlotte, North Carolina

Right: Conference room.
Below: Reception area.
Opposite: Work space.
Photography: Don Dubroff.

What company could simultaneously build a brand for the fifth largest bank in a region of giants, re-image a major medical center and create a kids' club for regional malls? Try Steedman Wilson, a lively, award-winning communications agency in Charlotte, North Carolina, founded in 1987 by president Toni Steedman. The firm's 6,000-square foot office, located in an 80-year-old warehouse in Charlotte's historic South End, was designed by Little Diversified Architectural Consulting (formerly Little & Associates Architects). The space, complete with exposed brick and wood beams, achieves two intriguing goals. It's a high-tech workplace with libraries and open teaming areas for productive thinking. And it's a flexible office where floor-to-ceiling walls are as reusable as furniture. "This space says we're smart and serious about what we do," Steedman explained, "but we also have fun doing it."

Little Diversified Architectural Consulting

Turnstone
e-Commerce Store and Showroom
Chicago, Illinois

Turnstone, a Steelcase company, is about making the workplace special. For ten years now, Turnstone has been offering furniture that is honest, flexible, affordable—and fun. And people seem to like it, because Turnstone keeps growing and adding new products all the time. To test a "bricks and clicks" selling environment, Turnstone opened its first e-commerce store and showroom, a playful 14,000 square foot space designed by Little Diversified Architectural Consulting (formerly Little & Associates Architects) on the ground floor of Chicago's

Merchandise Mart. The "living, breathing catalog" incorporates 12 display vignettes, a conference area, cash wrap, coffee bar and storage room, showcasing a flexible ceiling, raised floor and other devices that keep the vignettes, graphics and lighting fresh. Customers who like what they see can order online from computers in the store or from their offices or homes, possibly making Turnstone's "bricks and clicks" environment a dress rehearsal for the office furniture store of the future.

Above left: Window display.

Right: Cash wrap.

Opposite, top: Window displays.

Photography: Steelcase.

Little Diversified Architectural Consulting

Muzak Home Office
Fort Mill, South Carolina

Once "Background Music," now "Audio Architecture," Muzak creates experience with music. Understanding Muzak's need to promote its creative, cutting edge culture to their customers and employees and incorporate its new culture and brand within the new corporate headquarters, Little Diversified Architectural Consulting (formerly Little & Associates Architects) created an environment where the building and brand reflect one another. The environment, no less edgy and hip than Muzak sees itself, consists of a 100,000 square foot main floor and a 15,000 square foot mezzanine—calling for strong spatial orientation. Little responded with the equivalent of an urban space plan, creating a "city in a box" concept where the space was developed around a city center for company gatherings; the intimate heart of the city with a network of streets leading to more private spaces. The

Above: Main entry looking towards City Center.

Right: Open-plan work stations.

Opposite: City Center reception.

Photography: Peter Mauss/Esto Photographics.

team created a visual language, placing it into the environment in subtle but influential ways. The circle, a key part of Muzak's new identity, was sensitively integrated again and again. A non-hierarchical office environment was emphasized with identical office spaces for everyone from CEO William Boyd down. With the power to shape the experience of everyone that comes in contact with it, Muzak's Home Office is the perfect manifestation of its ultimate product: emotion.

Mancini·Duffy

39 West 13th Street
New York, NY 10011
212.938.1260
800.298.0868
212.938.1267 (Fax)
www.manciniduffy.com
info@manciniduffy.com

Washington, DC
Mountain Lakes
San Francisco
Stamford

Mancini·Duffy

Weil, Gotshal & Manges
Washington, DC

Office space near decision makers is coveted almost as much as access to decision makers in the nation's capital. So Mancini•Duffy was not surprised when the Washington, DC office of Weil, Gotshal & Manges, a respected law firm operating in the United States, Europe and Asia, enlisted it to create an efficient, 54,223-square foot, three-level facility downtown for some 52 attorneys and support staff serving national and international clients through a general regulatory practice. Two requirements drove the design. First, space allotted per attorney would be reduced to accommodate increased staff counts in less space than previously leased. Second, all meeting areas would be upgraded, and a conference center would be developed as the showpiece of the firm, featuring a multi-purpose, variable-size meeting room and a videoconferencing room. What is particularly satisfying about the design is that while space utilization drops from 850 to 750 square feet per attorney, the firm now has such attractive amenities as its conference center, library with coffee bar and dramatic interior staircase, along with private offices, support spaces, reception, catering area, pantry and restrooms—in this case, less being truly more.

Mancini·Duffy

NewView Technologies Inc.
New York, New York

Left: Elevator lobby.

Opposite, above: Reception.

Opposite, below left: Private offices.

Opposite, below right: Open meeting area.

Photography: Peter Paige.

One of the Internet's most compelling "killer applications" is the on-line auction exemplified by eBay, whose ability to create global markets for Hummel figurines and the like has made it a household name. Similarly, NewView Technologies, a New York-based supply chain management software company, was established to connect buyers and sellers of steel products in an open-bidding environment on the Internet. NewView retained Mancini•Duffy to create a 14,600-square foot, one-story space for its 47 employees that would appeal to employees as a supportive workplace and express the company's vision of "Steel meets the Internet." The solution uses open-plan work stations extensively, minimizes private offices, and celebrates steel in multiple forms. Indeed, the raw steel I-beams, stainless steel mesh and hardware, and weathered steel doors play well against finished concrete floors and exposed ceilings. The result: an exciting, high-tech, industrial look for executive offices, work stations, reception, boardroom, audio/visual presentation room and customer lounge—ready to move steel at Internet speed.

Mancini•Duffy   Exigen
San Francisco, California

How do you persuade customers to visit your demonstration center for enterprise software applications? Having great products is certainly one way. San Francisco-based Exigen has thrived by reducing the cost of service delivery operations, delivering business process improvement for industry-specific functions while lowering overall execution cost, risk and time to market. Having a state-of-the-art demonstration center, housed in a spectacular, 5,500-square foot penthouse designed by Mancini•Duffy with panoramic Bay Area views, helps too. The award-winning design places conference, dining and lounge areas in four glazed corners, uses the windowless infill for reception, support spaces, and two video presentation areas featuring multiple projectors, banquette seating and interactive lecterns/substations, and operates so efficiently that Exigen can conduct up to three customer presentations simultaneously, reconfiguring and sharing space as needed. Everything is articulated through a vocabulary of glass, wood, stainless steel and modern furnishings, forming a sleek, contemporary framework for viewing the City by the Bay.

Left: Suspended laminated glass door to conference room.

Below: Reception.

Opposite right: Wraparound corridor with view into client meeting room.

Opposite bottom left: Media presentation area.

Opposite bottom right: Conference room.

Photography: Cesar Rubio.

Mancini·Duffy

Airbus Industrie of North America
Herndon, Virginia

With 2,700 commercial passenger airliners in operation and orders for over 4,400 more, Airbus Industrie, a European aircraft manufacturer headquartered in Toulouse, France, has pulled abreast of Chicago-based Boeing, its chief rival and the world's longtime leader. Accordingly, its new, 45,000-square foot, two-level North American headquarters for some 120 employees in Herndon, Virginia, part of northern Virginia's high-tech corridor connecting Dulles International Airport and Washington, DC, has been designed by Mancini•Duffy to project an image befitting its stature and multi-national roots. As an extension of the Airbus "brand," the handsome, compact work environment of desk-based systems furniture is accented by "pods" of coffee bars and copy centers at major intersections that encourage staff interaction, and incorporates architectural elements that suggest aircraft contours. The two-story reception area was designed to display models of Airbus products and can be reconfigured to accommodate new models or product demonstrations for specific clients.

Above: View of reception from elevator lobby.

Right: Reception and stairway to upper level.

Photography: Michael Moran.

192

Margulies & Associates, Inc.

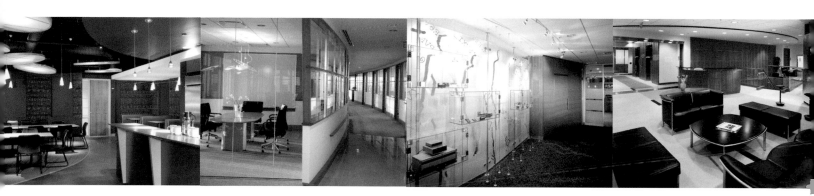

234 Congress Street
Boston, MA 02110
617.482.3232
617.482.0374 (Fax)
www.margulies.com

Margulies & Associates, Inc.

Lois Paul & Partners Headquarters
Woburn, Massachusetts

Above: Reception area.

Below left: Cyber cafe.

Below right: Casual conference area.

Opposite: Waiting area adjacent to main conference room.

Photography: Warren Patterson.

What could be more logical for a public relations and marketing firm in Boston, Austin and San Francisco serving high-tech, telecommunications and e-commerce companies than to resolve a complex spatial problem with a high-tech solution? For the new, 90,000-square foot, three-story headquarters of Lois Paul & Partners in Woburn, Massachusetts, designed by Margulies & Associates, the need to host regular company meetings and events requiring more space than any one room could justify inspired the creation of a suite of rooms designed to work separately and together. As a result, 257 employees in private offices and open-plan work stations enjoy access to such attractive, well-equipped and flexible building core support facilities as a cyber cafe, large meeting room/video conference room, other conference rooms and print center.

Margulies & Associates, Inc.

Oxford Bioscience Partners
Boston, Massachusetts

Some things are so good they must be shared. Take the magnificent views of Cambridge, Massachusetts, the Charles River, and Boston's Back Bay and Commons from the new, 15,000-square foot Boston office of Oxford Bioscience Partners, a life sciences venture capital firm. To offer these views to all 28 employees in a facility that includes a lounge/reception area, private and open-plan offices, conference center and cafe/kitchen, Margulies & Associates has designed an interior featuring an elegant, curving corridor wall of glass framed by hardwood and stainless steel that brings the outdoors inside. Oxford's office manager, Kathleen Moeckel, praises the designers, noting, "They listened carefully to our needs and responded with a layout that perfectly summarizes the culture we promote within our firm."

Above: Corridor.

Right: Waiting area and conference rooms.

Opposite: Reception desk.

Photography: Warren Patterson.

Margulies & Associates, Inc.

RSA Security
Corporate Headquarters
Bedford, Massachusetts

With over 9,000 customers around the globe, RSA Security is a strategic e-security partner to some of the largest and most successful companies using the Internet as part of their business strategy. Seeking an effective headquarters with an appropriate corporate identity for 1,000 employees, RSA recently engaged Margulies & Associates to fit out two new speculative office buildings in Bedford, Massachusetts as one, 320,000-square foot, four-story facility. The design establishes a powerful sense of openness and connectivity by cutting a three-story atrium/cafeteria into one building, placing a central spine and gathering "pods" on each floor, and erecting a pedestrian bridge that passes through the atrium and links the third floor spines of both buildings. The executive briefing center, private interior offices, open office areas, auditorium, cafeteria, fitness center and manufacturing constitute a memorable introduction to RSA.

Above: Conference "pod."

Below left: Display in executive briefing center.

Below right: Bridge joining Buildings One and Two.

Opposite: Lobby entrance and connecting stair.

Photography: Warren Patterson.

Margulies & Associates, Inc.

Forrester Research
Corporate Headquarters
Cambridge, Massachusetts

You won't find private offices at the new, Cambridge, Massachusetts headquarters of Forrester Research, a technology consulting firm that identifies and analyzes emerging trends in technology and their impact on business around the world from offices in Amsterdam, Austin, Cambridge, Frankfurt, London, San Francisco, Sydney and Tokyo. Forrester values interdisciplinary collaboration so highly that the 125,000-square foot, six-story facility for 480 employees, designed by Margulies & Associates, functions superbly as open workspaces called "pods" that are supported by casual and formal meeting areas, lunch room and game room. Whatever walls and doors do at Forrester, they don't block the flow of people and ideas.

Above: Reception desk.

Below left: Central reception area.

Below right: Elevator lobby.

Photography: Warren Patterson.

McMillan Group

25 Otter Trail
Westport
Connecticut 06880
203.227.8696
203.227.2898 (Fax)
info@mcmillangroup.com
www.mcmillangroup.com

McMillan Group

McMillan Group

Marconi Medical Systems Visitor Center
Highland Heights, Ohio

Right: Canopy and entrance.

Below: View of lobby with custom reception desk and seating alcove.

Opposite: View of lobby with motion graphic screen, interactive media tower and doorway to orientation theater.

Photography: Jamie Padgett/ Padgett and Company.

Who would buy a fine suit, European sedan or new home before seeing it in person? Seeing is believing, right? Interestingly, the customer for sophisticated medical imaging equipment agrees—and frequently makes the decision based on a trip to the manufacturer's briefing center. This revelation was critical for McMillan Group in designing the new, 20,000-square foot Marconi Medical Systems Visitor Center in Highland Heights, Ohio. The Center's mission was to establish a new identity for Picker International, a U.S. manufacturer of computed tomography (CT) scanners and other advanced health care equipment, as Marconi Medical Systems, a subsidiary of Marconi plc, the communications technology-

based successor to Britain's General Electric Co. To explain the transition from manufacturing to information technology, Marconi retained McMillan Group and Structura Architects to create a state-of-the-art demonstration center where customers could see its products as part of a total immersion experience. The linear journey each customer takes through the impressive, high-tech space starts in the grand lobby, where a light-filled rotunda's translucent, glowing media wall, and cylindrical media tower identify Marconi as a leading, high-tech medical company. From here, the customer heads to the orientation theater to watch a film on Marconi's capabilities,

steps past a disappearing glass wall into one of three demonstration rooms for interactive presentations, proceeds to view multimedia pedestals in the technology gallery, and winds up at one of four videoconferencing rooms. Customer response has been so favorable that Rob Spademan, a spokesman for Marconi (which recently sold the business to Philips Medical Systems, a subsidiary of Dutch conglomerate Royal Philips Electronics) declared, "Our new global Visitor Center has exceeded expectations on all levels."

Opposite: Videoconference room.

Above: Orientation theater.

Right: Demonstration room.

Below right: Technology gallery.

McMillan Group

Johnson Controls Inc.
Showcase for Building Environments
Brengel Technology Center
Milwaukee, Wisconsin

Left: Presentation Theatre.

Below: First floor building lobby with interactive displays.

Opposite: Reception desk in first floor lobby with portrait of Warren Johnson, founder of Johnson Controls.

Photography: Jamie Padgett/Padgett and Company.

Staying nimble after a century or more in business is a challenge for any company. Yet Milwaukee, Wisconsin-based Johnson Controls leads in its two core businesses, automotive systems and building controls, long after its founding by professor Warren Johnson in 1885. To maintain its prominence, the $20-billion corporation (2002 sales) has unveiled a new, 18,000-square foot customer business center in Milwaukee, designed by McMillan Group, working closely with Johnson Controls internal architectural department, to demonstrate its latest technologies and customer-based solu-

tions to buyers of automated building controls. How does the Showcase for Building Environments engage, inform and assure CEOs, CFOs and facility engineers of many Fortune 1000 companies, plus representatives of 7,000 school districts, more than 2,000 hospitals and tens of thousands of other non-residential and government buildings? McMillan Group designed the Showcase to unfold as a logical flow of space and information in the company's new Brengel Technology Center. Following a brief greeting in the 1st floor lobby, the customer goes to the 7th floor to see a presentation that begins

Left: Showcase lobby display on 7th floor.

Below left: Conference room overlooking Lake Michigan.

Below right: Orientation room transformed into the demonstration room set up.

with the orientation room's film and product display, continues with the presentation room's industry-based, multi-media programs, and concludes with discussions in two conference rooms and a customer dining room. The elegant, high-tech facility is not without such high-tech tools as white boards integrated with laptops, videoconferencing and advanced audio-visual systems, or such theatrical capabilities as weather effects that illustrate how Johnson Controls products can handle environmental changes and energy demands. However, there's also ample opportunity for live interaction with the company's technical experts—a reminder that Johnson Controls still knows what true leadership entails.

Mojo•Stumer Associates, P.C.

14 Plaza Road
Greenvale, NY 11548
516.625.3344
516.625.3418 (Fax)
www.mojostumer.com

Mojo•Stumer Associates, P.C.

We're Group
Jericho, New York

Above left: Boardroom.
Above right: Circulation spine.
Photography: Elliot Kaufman.

Sooner or later, the shoemaker's children get their shoes. For We're Group, a Jericho, New York merchant builder that designs, builds, owns and operates office properties, its new headquarters summarizes over 50 years and three genera-tions of family ownership. Accordingly, the facility's impressive, 8,000-square foot executive section, designed by Mojo-Stumer Associates, achieves effi-ciency and grace through economy and taste. Every space, from private offices, conference rooms and recep-tion to file storage, feels spacious and elegant. The reception area, for example, flows into the circulation spine to extend its area, while glass walls give pri-vate offices and conference rooms privacy and openness. We're Group loves the design, genuine praise from a developer of 10 million square feet of offices.

Left: Reception.
Right: Private office.

Mojo•Stumer Associates, P.C.

I-Park Lobby
Lake Success, New York

Few factories deserve footnotes in history, but the I-Park complex, a 1 million-square foot industrial campus in Lake Success, New York, does. As the home of Sperry Gyroscope, a navigational equipment manufacturer during World War II, the campus became the temporary headquarters for the United Nations in the late 1940s. The recent renovation of a 3,000-square foot lobby by Mojo-Stumer Associates contrasts the building's original flavor with a contemporary design in stainless steel, wood, terrazzo and glass, featuring a new reception desk, industrial finishes and a new column capital detail that illuminates the existing ceiling—and the past.

Above: Reception desk.

Below left: Cabinetry detail.

Below right: Column detail.

Opposite: Perspective with column capitals.

Photography: Carole Bates.

Mojo•Stumer Associates, P.C.

Related Management Company
New York, New York

Left: Exterior facade.

Below: Street level lobby reception desk.

Opposite: Stairwell to lower levels.

Photography: Elliot Kaufman.

Why would anyone wish to work in a windowless, underground space with no daylight, no views, and no other direct connection with the world at large? Underground space is indeed burdened with these obvious handicaps, but you actually might not find this troubling in the new, 15,000-square foot, three-story office in New York for 65 employees of Related Management Company, part of The Related Companies, one of the nation's leading developers, managers and financiers of premier real estate prop-

erties. As designed by Mojo-Stumer Associates, the private offices, open-plan office areas, conference rooms, lunchroom and file rooms were relocated from conventional accommodations elsewhere with the goal of creating a superior workplace regardless of the elevation. Light is brought as deeply as possible within the three-story stairwell that begins its descent at the street level lobby with a stone, metal and glass exterior facade and Lumacite stairwell wall. At the lower levels, numerous lighting

fixtures are employed to vary the quantity and quality of the light, creating the impression that daylight is entering via numerous paths. Light is then transmitted through arcades, clerestory windows and open plan work stations to illuminate what appears to be a clean, well-lighted and attractive place.

Above: Private offices with glass fronts.

Above right: Corridor leading to offices.

Right: Open plan office area.

Montroy Andersen Design Group, Inc.

432 Park Avenue South
New York, NY 10016
212.481.5900
212.481.7481 (Fax)
www.montroyandersen.com

Montroy Andersen Design Group, Inc.

Givaudan Fragrances Corp.
New York, New York

"That which we call a rose," Shakespeare observed in Romeo and Juliet, "by any other name would smell as sweet." But what if the smell were actually manufactured by Givaudan, one of the world's oldest and largest flavor and fragrance houses? Making perfumes and other substances smell like a rose is just one of the daily miracles performed by the Swiss company founded in 1895 by Leon and Xavier Givaudan in Zurich. Its commanding place in the global flavor and fragrance market has just been dramatized by an impressive, new facility in New York, where the company commissioned Montroy Andersen Design Group to design a 25,000-square foot "fine fragrance design studio." Here, customers evaluate products in an elegantly refined, multi-purpose space that combines a showroom, conference area, office and laboratory. The company and its design firm have created the effective selling environment by sending natural light deep into the office

Above: Reception area.

Right: View of laboratory from reception.

Opposite: Corridor with product display niches.

Photography: Paul Warchol.

Below: The unpartitioned conference area flows into the informal lounge, creating an inviting contrast to more structured spaces.

Opposite above: Private office.

Opposite right: Laboratory.

and laboratory through full-height glass partitions, and enriching the spacious and mostly open interiors with such fine building materials as hardwood veneers, decorative glass, hammered Jerusalem stone and stainless steel. Details count in this context. The laboratory, for instance, is positioned near the reception area so customers can easily observe technicians developing fragrances. Similarly, perfumes and evaluators are situated adjacent to the open conference area and informal lounge, while marketing and sales groups are located together in the resource library and work room to be readily available when needed. Currently headquartered in Vernier, Switzerland, Givaudan attributes its worldwide leadership to creating a "sensory advantage"™ for customers by combining vital aspects of nature, science, art and business to produce successful products. The smell of success is certainly in the air at Givaudan's New York studio.

Montroy Andersen Design Group, Inc.

Para Advisors
New York, New York

Left: Reception.

Below left: Conference room.

Photography: Phillip Ennis Studio.

It's no wonder financiers have responded to a global economy of instantaneous communications, rapid capital flows and universal access to information by largely abandoning their traditional milieu of 18th-century neoclassicism in favor of more contemporary settings. The spirit of finance today is more dynamic and less formal. That's why New York-based Para Advisors, a financial services firm, chose a contemporary image for its new, 6,500-square foot office, designed by Montroy Andersen Design Group. The space is open and inviting, surrounding staff and clients with warm, natural materials such as suede wallcoverings, slate, steel and cherry wood, metal and glass fronts to enclose perimeter offices, and furniture that blends with the wood trim and patterned carpet. However, a four-person trading desk occupies the center of the office, a reminder that transactions remain the essence of finance.

Montroy Andersen Design Group, Inc.

Bay Harbour Management
New York, New York

Privacy retains its subtle value in the workplace even as the volume of communications escalates. Thus, a major goal for the design of the new, 4,000-square foot office for Bay Harbour Management, a New York financial services firm, was to provide individual office space for all staff members without obstructing visual access. Montroy Andersen Design Group met the challenge by locating partitions with transparent and opaque glass elements along the curving perimeter of the centralized conference room, and placing the partners' space in the open area to maintain control and support—discreetly, of course.

Above: Conference room.
Left: Individual offices.
Photography: Paul Warchol.

Montroy Andersen Design Group, Inc.

Barry Bricken
New York, New York

Apparel industry veterans know how buyers' weeks affect showroom personnel and facilities, when large quantities of merchandise are presented to impatient retail buyers. Accordingly, designer Barry Bricken, whose classic, meticulously detailed womenswear and menswear sell through upscale catalogues, department stores, specialty shops and branded outlets, wanted versatility and efficiency in his new, 12,000-square foot New York showroom as well as a suitable atmosphere. Montroy Andersen Design Group created a handsome space dominated by movable walls that double as shelving units for storage and display, and added such details as cherry wood walls and shelving, frosted glass and spotlights for the finishing touches.

Above: Movable walls as shelving units.

Right: Reception.

Far right: View of multiple showroom spaces.

Photography: Geri Bauer Photographics, Inc.

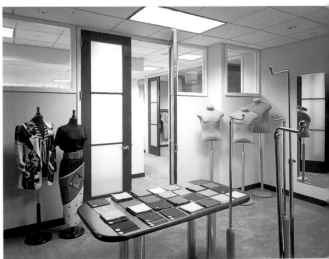

NELSON

The Nelson Building
222-30 Walnut Street
Philadelphia, PA 19106
215.925.6562
215.925.9151 (Fax)
www.nelsononline.com

Atlanta, GA
Baltimore, MD
Charlotte, NC
Chicago, IL
Dallas, TX
Ft. Lauderdale, FL
Hartford, CT
Jacksonville, FL
Minneapolis, MN
New York, NY
Providence, RI
Richmond, VA
San Francisco, CA
Shreveport, LA
St. Louis, MO
Tampa, FL
Wilmington, DE
Winston-Salem, NC

Wachovia Corporation
Charlotte, North Carolina

One can only imagine what Moravian settlers who named their tract in Charlotte, North Carolina "Wachovia" in 1753 to honor a Danube River valley, might think of Wachovia Corporation. Founded in 1879, Wachovia is now a financial giant with $342 billion in assets (December 31, 2002). To accommodate Wachovia's merger with First Union Bank, NELSON recently designed a versatile, high-tech, transitional-style executive office and conference center for 30 employees in a 20,000-square foot, two-story space. The sophisticated private offices, administrative work stations, conference rooms, lobby and support areas show clients a superbly illuminated portrait of the new Wachovia.

Above: Boardroom with oval-shaped table and suspended lighting ring.

Right: Conference room.

Far right: Administrative work stations.

Opposite: Prefunction area with pyramid ceiling cove.

Photography: Tim Buckman.

NELSON

Subaru of America
Operations Headquarters
Pennsauken, New Jersey

Faced with reusing former high-bay shop areas at Subaru of America Operations Headquarters in Pennsauken, New Jersey, as part of a 65,000-square foot, two-level renovation and addition of design studios, training spaces, locker rooms and more for 200 employees in the Japanese auto maker's existing building, NELSON has created a lively design that exploits the facility's volume and industrial origin. The result is a spacious, well-lit, open environment with exposed mechanical and electrical systems, an arrangement mirrored in remodeled office areas, where standard lay-in ceilings are deleted to compensate for tight floor-to-floor heights. Adaptability happens to be a virtue at Subaru, which produced its first car in 1955—38 years after Chikhei Nakajima founded the company as an aircraft manufacturer.

Above: Reception.

Right: Open-plan area.

Bottom right: Quiet room.

Left: Media room.

Photography: Peter Paige.

Although the Bank of America is one of the world's largest commercial banks, with 133,944 employees operating 4,208 banking centers in the United States and dozens more in over 150 countries, size was not the issue when the Bank and its affiliate, Banc of America Securities, lost their New York office at the World Trade Center on September 11, 2001. Fortunately, the Bank's determination to shelter its displaced personnel has resulted in a new, 180,000-square foot, two-level facility, developed in just six months. Once the Bank chose the former Manhattan Mall, a retail facility in the Herald Square district, it worked closely with NELSON to use the ample floors, which accommodate large business groups, 16-foot, 6-inch floor height, suitable for a new main computer center, roof and basement space, good locations for vital utilities, and interior atrium, a novel

Orlando Diaz-Azcuy Design Associates

Passersby could easily ignore the Courtside Athletic Club in Los Gatos, California for decades—until now. With a recent renovation and addition by Orlando Diaz-Azcuy Design Associates as interior designer and DES Architects and Engineers as architect, the structure has emerged as a stylish country club. The 87,400-square foot transformation has doubled floor area and refurbished or introduced tennis courts, fitness center, spa, childcare facility, teen center, pools, conference center and cafeteria, using such basic materials as terracotta, cement, wood, stucco and simple, heavy casual furniture. How do the 3,000 members feel about the changes? They've retained Diaz-Azcuy for the last 25 years.

Above: Lobby and concierge desk.

Opposite: Facade.

Photography: Matthew Millman (above), John Sutton (opposite).

Orlando Diaz-Azcuy Design Associates

Pacific Athletic Club
San Diego, California

Take an ideal site for an athletic club, a varied building program including exercise rooms, aerobics room, gymnasium, tennis courts, child care center, conference center and lunch room/cafe, a gracious neighborhood and an almost perfect climate, and you have the striking new Pacific Athletic Club in San Diego, featuring an interior design by Orlando Diaz-Azcuy Design Associates. The fact that the client, Western Athletic Clubs, has been developing such facilities for 25 years helps explain the excellent layout of the two-story space. Yet the sweeping, contemporary interior design of stone floors, stone and plaster walls, bamboo screens and fine furnishings nearly overwhelmed the client, who declared, "It's very impressive."

Top: Entrance lobby.
Oposite: Main stair.
Photography: Toshi Yoshimi.

Orlando Diaz-Azcuy Design Associates

Masa's Restaurant
San Francisco, California

San Francisco hails the reopening of Masa's, one of its most honored restaurants, serving a new menu from acclaimed chef Ron Siegel and a new 2,000-square foot interior from Orlando Diaz-Azcuy Design Associates. "Though the menus and the design signal a rebirth," Siegel explains, "Masa's still honors the original vision of chef Masataka Kobayashi to provide a truly amazing dining experience where contemporary French food, gracious service, and an elegant setting are all in sync." Even so, Masa's deep-red, Gilded Age look of 1983 has yielded to chocolate-brown walls, a white bar, white curtains, French toile chairs and a winning ambiance that's reassuring established patrons while attracting a younger clientele.

Photography: David Duncan Livingston.

OWP/P

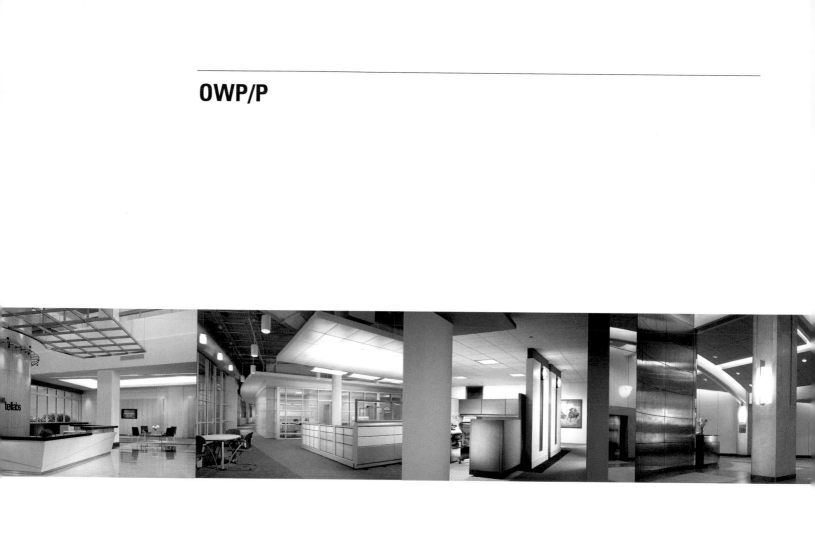

111 West Washington Street
Suite 2100
Chicago, IL 60602.2711
312.332.9600
312.332.9601 (Fax)
www.owpp.com

OWP/P

OWP/P

Left: Reception desk.

Below left: Retail space.

Below right: Breakout area.

Opposite: View of atrium facing "cafetorium."

Photography: Steve Hall @ Hedrich Blessing.

It's natural for Tellabs, a leading provider of bandwidth management solutions to telecommunications carriers around the world, to want its own employees to communicate as efficiently as possible. So when the company retained OWP/P to design its 850,000-square foot, 5-story headquarters for 2,300 employees in Naperville, Illinois, it developed a handsome new facility that is unusually fluid, informal and responsive. Ninety-nine percent of office space is open plan to facilitate the reorganization of internal groups and encourage open communications between teams. A two-story atrium, the formal entry point for both employees and visitors, adds such support facilities as a range of informal and formal meeting areas, demonstration laboratory, photography studio, servery, 750-seat "cafetorium," fitness center and retail space to collectively demonstrate why Tellabs is essential to metro/regional communications networks in over 100 countries.

OWP/P

Sauer-Danfoss, Inc.
Executive Office
Lincolnshire, Illinois

Effective administration is a logistic challenge even for leading international organizations. Consider the problem recently faced by Sauer-Danfoss, one of the world's largest manufacturers and suppliers of hydrostatic transmissions, steering components, motors, valves, open circuit products and electrohydraulic controls. Because the small, separate offices previously occupied by about 10 company executives and their staff acted as an impediment to directing some 7,000 employees in the Americas, Europe and the Asia-Pacific region, OWP/P designed one 12,600-square foot executive office for them on a C-shaped floor plate in Lincolnshire, Illinois. Its ample open areas for teaming, private offices with glass walls, main conference room, videoconferencing room, library and copy/mail center now give Sauer-Danfoss's leaders a compelling workplace to share.

244

OWP/P

Fujisawa Healthcare, Inc. Headquarters
Deerfield, Illinois

When in Rome, do as the Romans. In Deerfield, Illinois, Fujisawa Healthcare, Inc., a North American subsidiary of Osaka, Japan-based Fujisawa Pharmaceutical Company Ltd., has shifted from a hierarchical organization to a less formal, more collaborative culture. The consequences have shaped its newly remodeled, 130,000-square foot, 4-story headquarters, designed by OWP/P for 308 employees. A floor restacking to promote openness, color-coded work stations, walls and carpet that assist wayfinding, circulation patterns offering greater access to executives, new social spaces for informal teaming, enhanced teleconferencing capabilities and Internet access, and better coffee break areas and other amenities for easy interaction subtly acknowledge Fujisawa's locale.

Above left: Open-plan office area.

Above right: Reception.
Left: Conference room.

Photography: Craig Dugan @ Hedrich Blessing.

One North Dearborn
Chicago, Illinois

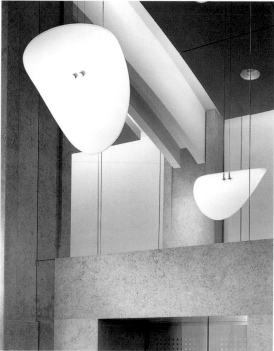

One reason why Chicago businesses find One North Dearborn an attractive address in a competitive market—aside from the obvious point about location, location, location—is that MB Real Estate, a major Chicago property owner, recently completed an extensive technological upgrade and architectural renovation with OWP/P that has re-energized the one million-square foot structure.

Though One North Dearborn's original design concept endures, the renovation has transformed exterior walls, core elements for 11 50,000-square foot office floors, and elevator cab interiors, as well as overall infrastructure. Even the lobby, its mezzanine yielding to a dramatic, two-story arched ceiling, is soaring to new heights and taking Chicagoans along.

Above left: Lobby perspective with concierge desk and elevators.

Above right: Custom lighting details.

Right: Semi-circular suspended ceiling panel at corridor intersection.

Photography: Chris Barrett @ Hedrich Blessing.

OWP/P

Congress Center
Chicago, Illinois

Left: Lobby reception desk.

Above: Street elevation of lobby.

Below: Elevator lobby.

Photography: Steve Hall @ Hedrich Blessing.

There's a new face among the icons of American architecture in Chicago's West Loop. Congress Center is a 529,000-square foot, 16-story office building designed by OWP/P for Development Resources, Inc. to meet tenants' needs for advanced technology. Developed under a limited budget and aggressive timetable that used pre-cast concrete on the east and west facades and curtain-wall on the north and south facades for simultaneous erection and reduced construction time, it offers surprises nonetheless. Each 33,000-square foot floor is column-free, and public spaces, often overlooked in speculative development, feature floating ceiling that nobody will overlook.

Partridge Architects, Inc.

1617 JFK Boulevard
Suite 900
Philadelphia, PA 19103
215.567.3595
215.557.7984 (Fax)
www.partridgearch.com

Partridge Architects, Inc.

Domus, Inc.
Philadelphia, Pennsylvania

Businesses who want customized service, rapid response and delivery, and cost effectiveness in communicating with customers will find Philadelphia-based Domus, Inc. a pleasant surprise. This full-service marketing communications agency combines in-house strategic planning and account management with a national network of top independent creative, research and media talent to assemble customized account teams for clients. Not surprisingly, Domus's fresh approach is also displayed in its new, 11,000-square foot, two-level office, designed by Partridge Architects, for some 45 employees. Originally designed to anticipate its current expansion, the facility handles relatively inexpensive materials with efficiency and creativity to create the kind of memorable impact that clients like Aramark, Con-Agra, Fisher-Price, Mannington Floors, Novo Nordisk Pharmaceuticals and Wawa Food Markets have come to expect.

Partridge Architects, Inc.

McCarter & English, LLP
Philadelphia, Pennsylvania

Recognized as a litigation powerhouse, McCarter & English has earned a national reputation over the past 150 years as legal counsel for leading companies in the pharmaceutical, chemical and medical device industries. Enhancing this enviable track record is one of the objectives of the firm's new, 26,000-square foot Philadelphia office, designed by Partridge Architects, for 16 attorneys and a staff of about 50. The heart of the facility, which includes private offices, secretarial work stations, reception and elevator lobby, is its impressive conference center, incorporating seven rooms in various sizes, including one that accommodates the entire work force. But the scheme leaves nothing to chance. Once visitors enter the elegant, traditional "front office" of cherry millwork, entrances of etched, beveled glass set in wood-framed doors and sidelights, and matching, transitional-style furnishings, they know exactly where they are.

Above left: Elevator lobby.
Above right: Reception.
Left: Main conference room.
Opposite: Small conference room.
Photography: Matt Wargo Photography.

252

Partridge Architects, Inc.

Dorland Global Communications
Philadelphia, Pennsylvania

Above: Reception.

Left: View from stairwell to reception.

Opposite: Server room as seen from staircase.

Photography: Matt Wargo Photography.

If you stop by the new, ruggedly handsome, 30,000-square foot, two-level office of Dorland Global Health Communications for 90 employees in an historic Philadelphia building, designed by Partridge Architects, you may not realize that Dorland is the second oldest advertising agency in continuous operation in the United States, founded in 1883. Yet you might be alerted to the fact that award-winning Dorland consistently ranks as one of the nation's top 30 advertis-

ing and public relations agencies specializing in health care, as well as its largest independent health-care agency. All this is fine with Dorland. The agency deliberately sought a youthful, industrial look that would encourage employee interaction, exchange of ideas and teamwork in serving such prestigious clients as Cephalon, Chiron, duPont Hospital for Children, and Roche Molecular Systems. Accordingly, the designers created a distinctive ambiance for the private

offices, open-plan work stations, conference rooms with pantry, IT room and large gathering area that features polished concrete floors, exposed ceilings, plumbing, cable trays and air ducts, dramatic lighting, such timeless modern furnishings as Breuer's Wassily chair, and a convenient sculptural staircase of oak and steel that could double as a work of art.

Above: Detail of staircase's oak and steel construction.

Left: Gathering space for meetings, pantry and parlor games.

Right: "Red Wall" enclosing library and small conference area.

Perkins & Will

800.837.9455
gary.wheeler@perkinswill.com
www.perkinswill.com

Atlanta
Beijing
Boston
Charlotte/RTP
Chicago
Dallas
Houston
Los Angeles
Miami
Minneapolis
New York
Shanghai

Perkins & Will

Tribune Interactive
Chicago, Illinois

Above left: Lounge.

Above right: Main circulation corridor.

Right: Railing detail.

Opposite: Perspective of conference and training rooms.

Photography: Steven Hall, Hedrich-Blessing Photography.

Who would expect to enter a Gothic Revival structure in Chicago's River North district, descend to sub-grade floors that once housed the Chicago Tribune's pressroom, and find a bright and accessible high-tech workplace? Welcome to the 94,000-square foot, three-story office of Tribune Interactive, the online division of Tribune Co., publisher of the Chicago Tribune. To foster collaboration, improve communications and encourage creativity, Tribune Interactive retained Perkins & Will to create a flexible and technologically advanced environment for its 250 employees, who were dispersed over 10 floors of the landmark 1925 Tribune Tower. Amidst massive concrete pillars supporting the tower above, the design places open work stations and conference and training rooms and hoteling spaces, along with a 12,500-square foot, two-story fitness center for all Tribune employees. Greater operational efficiency and a new cultural identity have promptly made the new facility as popular with employees as Tribune Interactive's services—via print, radio, Web and TV—are with customers.

Perkins & Will

Fallon Worldwide
Minneapolis, Minnesota

Nothing launches advertising agencies faster than brilliant, creative ideas. Indeed, the spark of creativity still blazes at the new, 145,000-square foot, three-story office of Fallon Worldwide in Minneapolis, Minnesota, designed by Perkins & Will for 400 employees. On the strength of such acclaimed work as Holiday Inn's "Mark" campaign, Prudential's "Be Your Own Rock" campaign, and Nuveen Investment's

Christopher Reeve spot, Fallon has grown from five individuals who founded Fallon McElligott in 1981 into a global concern with New York and London branches—the second global network for France's Publicis Group—billing almost $1 billion annually. Has success spoiled Fallon? Judging from the new environment, supporting a business model of brand teams, emphatically no. Space is organized into

independent, open-plan neighborhoods where brand teams assigned to universal work stations remain visually connected to each other, individuals move about along paths anchored by sophisticated conference rooms and skylit, three-story internal staircases, and brands such as BMW, Lee Jeans and MTV are flourishing.

RMW architecture & interiors

Wharton School of Business
Wharton West Center
San Francisco, California

Go West! Believing it is never too late to heed Horace Greeley's famous advice, the prestigious Wharton School, founded at the University of Pennsylvania in 1881 as the nation's first collegiate business school, recently opened its first permanent location outside Philadelphia in San Francisco's SOMA district. Wharton West now offers executive MBA (WEMBA) and non-degree executive education programs in a sophisticated, 20,000-square foot space, designed by RMW architecture & interiors, on the fifth floor and mezzanine of the historic Folger Building, a 1905 warehouse. Of course, the two 60-seat tiered classrooms, breakout rooms, study rooms, faculty and administrative offices, serving pantry and dining room have their fair share of advanced technology, including Internet2 service, the latest audio-visual and video conferencing equipment, and state-of-the-art building mechanical and electrical systems. But since WEMBA students fly in from various domestic and foreign locations to attend classes every other weekend for two years, the contemporary environment is appointed in solid, comfortable furnishings. And by faculty request, there are old-fashioned chalkboards too.

Left: View from mezzanine.

Above: Breakout room.
Top: Reception.

Opposite: Stairwell.

Photography: Ethan Kaplan
©2002.

RMW architecture & interiors

Hewlett Packard
Executive Briefing Center
Cupertino, California

Below: Reception area.

Opposite, upper left:
Entrance.

Opposite, upper right:
Exterior.

Photography:
Sharon Risedorph ©2001;
Ethan Kaplan ©2001 (bottom
right).

A lot has happened to the legendary business founded in 1939 by Stanford University engineering graduates William Hewlett and David Packard. To meet the new Hewlett Packard, which merged with Compaq Computer in May 2002, corporate customers for its computers, printers and other products and services are invited to an "immersive" experience at the newly renovated, 40,000-square foot Executive Briefing Center in Cupertino, California, designed by RMW architecture & interiors. Among the interactive exhibits, 12 briefing rooms, three track presentation rooms, theater, two executive suites and e-cafe, HP's capabilities are displayed through a sophisticated audio-visual, data and telecommunications infrastructure that is imaginatively integrated with a sleek, modern architecture of limestone, stainless steel and wood—a working vision of the 21st century.

Above: View of theater from reception.
Right: Interactive showroom.

RMW architecture & interiors

Gray Cary Ware & Freidenrich LLP
San Francisco, California

For a leading and decidedly non-traditional law firm representing emerging growth and technology companies, Gray Cary Ware & Freidenrich LLP has a bold new, 57,000-square foot, two-story San Francisco office for 84 attorneys and a support staff of 34, designed by RMW architecture & interiors, to match its practice. The facility, located in a new building across the street from Pacific Bell Park, home of the San Francisco Giants, has raised access flooring, under-floor air distribution and an open, loft-like space that has been adapted to provide modular private offices for attorneys and paralegals, open areas beneath dropped soffits for secretaries and a dramatic, two-story reception area serving the entire staff. Judging from the vitality of this office, the rapid growth of the 420-attorney firm during the last three years seems far from over.

Left: Interior stair.

Far left: Secretarial area.

RNL Design

Colorado Springs Utilities Headquarters
Colorado Springs, Colorado

Talk gets serious in the West when anyone mentions water, which Westerners have contested since the region was settled in the latter half of the 19th century. For example, Colorado Springs, Colorado bought its first water rights to irrigate trees just a year after it was founded by General William J. Palmer in 1871. Appreciating the ongoing importance of water, electricity and gas, Colorado Springs Utilities emphasizes reliability, value and community service in dealing with 569,122 customers (2002), and celebrates these values in its new, 70,000-square foot, four-story headquarters for 300 employees, designed by RNL Design as part of a 10-year contract with the publicly-owned corporation. The design uses the warm, inviting and user-friendly private and open-plan offices, boardroom and reception area, appointed in basic building materials accented by cherry wood millwork and slate flooring, curving walls and ceilings that contrast with an orthogonal grid, and a dramatic blend of man-made lighting and daylight transmitted through interior glass walls to assure employees and customers alike that they are valued as much as water.

Ask Dilbert. Even cartoonist Scott Adams' harried office nerd would admit that modern offices need both private offices and "cube farms" or open-plan areas. The dynamics between the environments help explain the visual appeal and operating success of the new, 30,207-square foot corporate office for 110 employees of Agilera in Englewood, Colorado, designed by RNL Design. Agilera, a full-service application service provider, wanted a distinctive workplace that one executive described as "professional funk"—a classic look with a twist. The private and open-plan offices, network operations center, training room, break room, reception area and conference center achieve this goal through such playful juxtapositions as straight walls versus canted, curved and cut-out ones, exposed ceilings versus suspended soffits, earth tones versus primary colors, and direct versus indirect lighting. Adding to the fun is the folding, "garage"-style overhead door dividing training and break facilities, which does what you would expect whenever the whole staff gathers.

Above: Private and open-plan offices.

Right: Reception.

Opposite, above left: Break room.

Photography: Edward LaCasse.

Roger Ferris + Partners

PanAmSat World Headquarters
Wilton, Connecticut

Right: Boardroom and lounge.
Below left: Reception desk.
Below right: Reception seating.
Bottom: Main corridor.
Opposite: Teleconference room.
Photography: Woodruff & Brown.

Buck Rogers, Captain Kirk and Luke Skywalker are nowhere in sight at PanAmSat's handsome new, 75,000-square foot headquarters in Wilton, Connecticut, designed by Roger Ferris + Partners. Then again, being the satellite-based communications pioneer that launched the world's first privately owned international satellite in 1984, as well as an industry powerhouse fielding 22 satellites with over 900 usable transponders, 700-plus employees, seven technical ground facilities and 13 offices on five continents, PanAmSat is serious about its role as a leading distributor of entertainment and information. As a result, its executive offices, program support rooms, boardroom and teleconference rooms constitute a contemporary workplace of maple wood, carpet and glass that is sophisticated yet understated, where 254 employees serve a network reaching 98 percent of the world's population.

Roger Ferris + Partners

Sempra Energy Trading Expansion
Stamford, Connecticut

The clear spans and high ceiling suited the 100-position trading floor and support facility needed by Sempra Energy Trading® Corp., a subsidiary of Sempra Energy, a Fortune 500 energy services holding company. But as one of North America's largest energy trading companies, Sempra wanted the 1940s brick warehouse in Stamford, Connecticut, to project an appropriate image, and worked with Roger Ferris + Partners a few years ago to achieve that. Now, Sempra and Ferris have expanded the original, 40,000 square feet to 120,000 square feet to equip 250 employees with a new trading room, private and open offices, conference rooms, boardroom, kitchen and support facilities, backed by robust infrastructure. The facility's innovations include its design, introducing a 5-degree rotation in the building grid for new construction that begins with the curtain wall and concludes with an open interior of exposed ceilings and mechanical systems outfitted with maple wood, aluminum and glass—a powerhouse for 21st-century commerce.

Top right: Private offices.

Upper right: Entrance.

Above right: Reception.

Left: Trading room.

Opposite: Perimeter of trading room.

Photography: Michael Moran.

Roger Ferris + Partners

AIG Trading
London, United Kingdom

Right: Trading room.

Lower left: Reception.

Bottom left: Conference room.

Opposite lower right: Private office.

Photography: Michael Moran.

Ceilings rarely attract attention. Yet what's above the 150 employees of AIG Trading Group in a new, 40,000-square foot, two-level trading facility in London's St. Katherine's district, designed by Roger Ferris + Partners, took great care to rearrange. Since unobstructed space is required in all trading rooms, Greenwich, Connecticut-based AIG Trading, which engages in trading and market making in foreign exchange, emerging markets, precious and base

metals, energy and commodity indices, had to remove three columns on the top two floors of an office tower for its growing London operations. This involved transferring the weight of the roof and the building's mechanical equipment to deep girders and isolating the equipment to contain vibration. The engaging design has been completed with indirectly lighted ceiling coffers, metal and glass partitions, beech wood trim and contemporary furnishings and raised flooring to surround employees with light and views they are sure to notice.

Roger Ferris + Partners

Cena Restaurant
New York, New York

Left: Facing the main dining room from the street.

Above: Lounge.

Below left: Bar.

Cena, hailed by New York Times restaurant critic Ruth Reichl as one of the "most promising" of New York's latest eateries when it opened, was designed by Roger Ferris + Partners to transform two deep and narrow, 5,000-square foot floors into a spacious, sunny and sophisticated oasis for fine dining in the Chelsea neighborhood. Indeed, indirect uplighting, backlit glass column capitals, a glazed street level facade and a finely tailored, contemporary interior of stainless steel, birdseye maple, glass tile, etched glass, Venetian plaster and stylish furniture worked their magic. The main dining area, private dining area, bar, wine room, kitchen, prep kitchens, reception area, lounge and restrooms positively glowed—as did the New Yorkers who flocked to Cena's acclaimed Italian cuisine.

RTKL

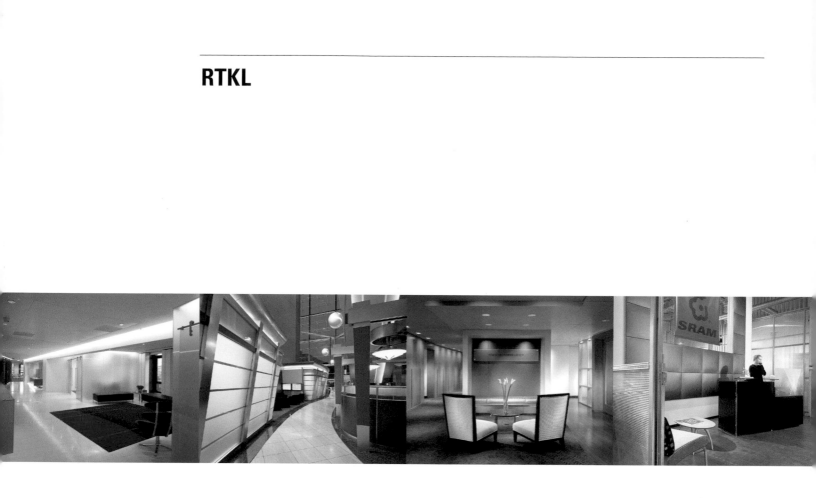

Baltimore
410.528.8600

Dallas
214.871.8877

Washington
202.833.4400

Los Angeles
213.627.7373

Chicago
312.704.9900

Denver
303.824.2727

Miami
786.268.3200

London
44.207.306.0404

Tokyo
81.33583.3401

Shanghai
86.21.6279.7657

Madrid
34.91.426.0980

www.rtkl.com

RTKL

Reed Smith Warner Cranston
London, United Kingdom

Above: Foyer.

Below left: Meeting room.

Below right: Private office.

Photography: Morley von Sternberg.

It started with a word game. To develop a new London office for Reed Smith Warner Cranston, the British arm of Reed Smith, a Pittsburgh-based law firm with over 700 attorneys in America and the United Kingdom, RTKL Associates, designer of the 30,000-square foot, three-level space, asked senior partners for buzz words to describe their firm's strategic vision. Words like "entrepreneurial," "alternative" and "commercial" were incorporated into the design brief. Thus,

when RSWC's 60 attorneys and a support staff moved into the new facility, they found an environment designed for open communications, operational transparency, accessibility and friendliness. Modular floor plans, glazed office fronts and an uncomplicated furniture system maintain flexibility and maximize exposure to spectacular views of The Thames, The Golden Hinde, Southwark Cathedral and London Bridge from private window offices, open-plan work stations, meeting rooms, public/lobby spaces and staff canteen/cafe. Commenting on the installation, Mark Dembovsky, chief strategic officer for RSWC, declared, "It feels and looks great. This is so us."

Above: Reception area.

RTKL

Shinsei Bank
Tokyo, Japan

Can a Japanese bank succeed by addressing customers' needs with diversified services and paying attention to profitability? In a nation where banks often resemble cash machines for favored corporate borrowers, this Western approach to banking is the credo of Shinsei Bank, the reincarnation of Long-Term Credit Bank of Japan (shinsei means "rebirth"), which American investors took over in 2000. Concurrent with the restructuring of its management team, business plans, IT platforms and operating procedures, Shinsei retained

RTKL Associates to create a stylish and user-friendly new environment for its 800-square meter (8,608-square foot) flagship retail bank that is transforming its 25 branches through a kit-of-parts program, and its Meguro Call Center. The contrast between a Shinsei retail installation and those of competing institutions is striking. Everything from credit cards to kiosks reflects a personal touch that functionally and visually appeals to customers, offering personal banking stations instead of the standard long counter, customer service

representatives, and a coffee bar for latte and information on banking services. While the fate of Japan's second-largest credit bank will take months to determine, Shinsei gives credibility to the notion that customer service and profits should be touchstones of modern banking in Japan.

Top: Flagship individual consulting spaces.

Above: Call center rest area.

Below left: Flagship consultation area.

Below right: Call center employee cafe.

Opposite: Flagship exterior.

Photography: Toshio Kaneko

RTKL

The Schinnerer Group, Inc. Headquarters
Chevy Chase, Maryland

Here's a recipe for disaster. Combine noise, vibration, debris, displacement and office work, and stir well. Yet occupied offices can be remodeled successfully, as shown by RTKL Associates in its meticulous, seven-phase, 48-week renovation of a 65,000-square foot space for the Chevy Chase, Maryland headquarters of The Schinnerer Group, Inc., the nation's leading underwriting manager of professional liability lines since 1947. When the project was completed recently, a dark, unfocused and inefficient warren of private offices gave way to an open, structured and flexible space. The new, daylight-saturated environment features private offices in the interiors, open-plan areas on the perimeters, and such amenities as teaming areas, cafes and conveniently located, centralized services. Observed Schinnerer's president, Vincent Santorelli, "Our people are delighted with the results."

Left: Conference room.

Below: Reception area.

Opposite, upper left: Entrance.

Opposite, lower left: Employee cafe.

Photography: Jeffrey Jacobs.

THE SCHINNERER GROUP

RTKL

SRAM Headquarters
Chicago, Illinois

Left: Reception.

Below left: Test track.

Below center: Multi-purpose layout.

Right: Individual work station.

Photography: Christopher Barrett/Hedrich-Blessing.

Cycling enthusiasts can appreciate why SRAM, a global bicycle components manufacturer with facilities in Europe and Asia, wanted the new, 35,000-square foot Chicago headquarters to let its 65 employees "do what they've always done." As the source of such respected components as Grip Shift® shifters, ESP® derailleurs and Spectro™ internal gear hubs, and a major supplier to such leading bicycle brands as Cannondale, Diamond Back, GT, Schwinn, Specialized, Trek, and Univega, SRAM is a major force in cycling. Accordingly, RTKL Associates worked closely with the manufacturer to create a high-performance, team-oriented and "intellectual-cool" environment where employees would thrive. With a 650-foot oval test track that doubles as primary circulation path as its heart, the new workplace is characterized by reconfigurable work stations, developed with SRAM's product development group, where research, design, testing, manufacturing and administration occur side by side, and such amenities as locker rooms, showers and bicycle storage for the largely bicycle-riding staff. Cool indeed.

Sasaki Associates, Inc.

64 Pleasant Street
Watertown, MA 02472
617.926.3300
617.924.2748 (Fax)
info@sasaki.com
www.sasaki.com

900 North Point Street
Suite B300
San Francisco, CA 94109
415.776.7272
415.202.8970 (Fax)
sanfrancisco@sasaki.com

Sasaki Associates, Inc.

Seyfarth Shaw
Boston, Massachusetts

Pragmatic, egalitarian and progressive are descriptions that seem surprisingly apt in the new, 33,000-square foot Boston office for 91 employees of Seyfarth Shaw, a law firm employing some 500 attorneys in nine offices throughout the nation and one in Brussels. Founded in 1945 by three attorneys, the firm honors its origins by maintaining one of the nation's largest labor and employment practices, along with legal services in such areas as business law, contracts and litigation. The dynamic Boston branch, designed by Sasaki Associates, distinguishes itself through flexible, same-size attorneys' offices (160 square feet) with French doors that open to the interior, an exposed ceiling structure that creates interest and considerable overhead volume, and handsome furnishings which nonetheless value efficiency over image. Frequent tours suggest that Boston's attorneys are getting the message.

Above: Arched window at main conference room.

Left: Private office.

Right: Conference room.

Lower right: Secretarial stations.

Opposite: Elevator lobby.

Photography: Lucy Chen.

Sasaki Associates, Inc.

Cabot Corporation
Boston, Massachusetts

Right: Elevator lobby.

Lower left: Executive conference area.

Lower right: CPort Cafe.

Bottom right: One-size private office.

Opposite: Informal conference space.

Photography: Lucy Chen.

In a refreshing departure from tradition, Cabot Corporation, a $1.5+ billion global specialty chemicals company headquartered in Boston, has returned to its founding as a manufacturer in 1882 to inspire a new, 66,000-square foot, two-story corporate office, designed by Sasaki Associates for 160 employees. The result is spartan, versatile and even exhilarating in its celebration of industry. Interconnecting steps mimic ships' gangways, an overhead garage door encloses an executive conference area, exposed ceilings reveal their "guts," and concrete block and drywall painted in saturated tones displace mahogany and granite. Reminders that Cabot's fortunes have depended on more than its executives are proudly featured, including graphic displays about the company and its products, one-size, 140-square foot offices, and a cafeteria with a harbor view that doubles as a town square. To quote a visiting employee, "It's young for an old company. Great job!"

Sasaki Associates, Inc.

TJX Companies Headquarters
Framingham, Massachusetts

Left: Cafe-style seating overlooks atrium.

Right: The salad bar at the servery's center.

Photography: Lucy Chen.

Today, nobody wants to pay "manufacturer's suggested retail price" or MSRP in America. It's the perfect retail climate for TJX, a leading off-price retailer of apparel and home fashions, which operates T.J. Maxx, Marshalls, HomeGoods and A.J. Wright in the United States, Winners and HomeSense in Canada, and T.K. Maxx in Europe. Rigorous growth in TJX's divisions has resulted in the addition of 800 associates and a 300,000-square foot building, interiors designed by Sasaki Associates, to the company's headquarters in Framingham, Massachusetts. To assure the efficiency of the 800,000-square foot complex of three five-story buildings, TJX also asked Sasaki to develop a master plan and updated design concept, along with renovations of the existing executive area and cafeteria. TJX wisely insisted the cafeteria, enlarged to accommodate the latest associates, provide an escape from the workplace. The delightful new outdoor market ambiance does just that.

Left: Servery features a pizza oven.

Right: Associates of the Month.on the wall beyond the registers.

Photography: Lucy Chen.

Sasaki Associates, Inc.

Biogen Inc.
Cambridge, Massachusetts

Left: The reception desk's sight-lines cover the entire center.

Photography: Lucy Chen

As the world's oldest independent biotechnology company, Biogen, founded in 1978 by renowned scientists to discover and develop new drugs through genetic engineering, takes pride in maintaining a superior work environment. Its fast-track development of a new, 6,500-square foot fitness center on its Cambridge, Massachusetts campus, designed by Sasaki Associates, shows why the company is respected for such products as Avonex® (Interferon beta-1a) for treatment of relapsing forms of multiple sclerosis. Enlisting Sasaki and its contractor to team with company representatives in an interactive design process and value engineering, Biogen was able to deliver a project on time and cost that is also a joy to see and use.

SCR Design Organization, Inc.

305 East 46th Street
New York, NY 10017
212.421.3500
212.220.8869 (Fax)

www.scrdesign.com
info@scrdesign.com

4F, Building B, 357 Zhaohua Road
Shanghai, P.R.C. 200050
8621.6251.1398
8621.6251.1358 (Fax)

9-20 Qinghua East Road
Beijing, P.R.C. 100083
8610.6232.9135
8610.6231.9027 (Fax)

Affiliates in Principal Cities of the World

SCR Design Organization, Inc.

Investment Banking Company
New York, New York

Above: Trading room.
Right: Town center.
Photography: Peter Paige.

Having received a Five-Star Certification Award from a major investment banking company for over a decade of exemplary service, value, communication and professionalism, SCR Design Organization knows the virtue of consistency. Yet in providing planning and design services for more than 750,000 square feet of the brokerege offices, SCR can point to various assignments that deliberately break the mold. Shown here are two projects, one a private client service space that exhibits corporate class and dignity. The other project shown is the new 70,000-square foot, two-story space for 400 employees of the bank's online trading operations. Its heart is a two-story high town center equipped with a cafe servery for light lunches, 24-hour snack bar, pool table, video game area and wide-screen TVs. Who says consistency leaves no room for a delightful surprise or two?

Above: Elevator lobby.

Right: Reception.

SCR Design Organization, Inc.

Pfizer Howmedica
Rutherford, New Jersey

The operation must have sounded familiar to Pfizer Howmedica, a leading worldwide supplier of joint implants for bone replacement procedures. To develop Howmedica's new, 18,000-square foot executive headquarters and conference center for 50 employees from an existing L-shaped building in Rutherford, New Jersey, SCR Design Organization would insert a new rotunda at the bend in the "L." The renovation neatly splits the structure into two functional zones and creates a focal point for visitors. Such features as a circular, maple-paneled reception area within a glass-enclosed rotunda, cherry wood-paneled executive offices, state-of-the-art conference rooms, and a new exterior introducing stucco panels and a vaulted roof that brings daylight indoors complete the successful "procedure."

Above left: Executive office suite.

Above right: Exterior with new rotunda.

Left: General office area.

Opposite: Reception area within rotunda.

Photography: Peter Paige.

Left: Main conference room and adjoining lounge.

Top right: Typical corridor.

Below: Trading floor.

Photography: Peter Paige.

Recovering quickly from the trauma of September 11, 2001 was not an option for many New York City businesses—it was a dire necessity. One such enterprise was Sandler O'Neill & Partners, LP, an investment banking firm specializing in the management of IPOs, bond trading and equities research for banks and thrifts which lost employees in the destruction of its headquarters on the 104th floor of the World Trade Center. With no time to lose, SCR Design Organization helped Sandler O'Neill as the firm secured new space in October 2001, relocated to temporary space in November 2001, and occupied its new, 28,000-square foot, midtown Manhattan headquarters in January 2002. The new reception area, state-of-the-art trading floor, multi-media conference area, private offices and administrative work stations for the staff of 150 are quietly assuring. The neutral color palette of white walls, gray and brown furnishings, natural maple millwork and glass, complemented by artwork by Roy Lichtenstein and Andy Warhol, appropriately offers no hint of the project's urgency.

SCR Design Organization, Inc.

Knight Trading Group, Inc.
Jersey City, New Jersey

Years before the attack on New York's World Trade Center, the New Jersey shore of the Hudson River facing lower Manhattan was already booming as an adjunct to New York's financial center. A good example of Wall Street thriving in the Garden State is Knight Trading Group, an international brokerage firm known as Knight/Trimark Group until May 2000. Knight, a client of SCR Design Organization since its founding in 1995, had expanded to the point that it recently asked SCR to design a new, 270,000-square foot headquarters in a build-to-suit property in Jersey City. The result—embracing two 25,000-square foot trading floors with over 1,000 trading positions and executive offices nearby, general office space arrayed in teaming clusters, glass-enclosed network operations center, 250-seat cafeteria, 100-person auditorium and data center backed by UPS/generator system—is New Jersey-based and decidedly world-class.

Above: Cafeteria.
Left: General office space.
Below: Elevator lobby.
Photography: Peter Paige.

Silvester + Tafuro, Inc.

50 Washington Street
South Norwalk, CT 06854
203.866.9221
203.838.2436 (Fax)

Silvester + Tafuro, International
Unit 7, 2nd Floor
Culvert House
Culvert Road
Battersea, London SW11 SAP
United Kingdom
44.207.498.5534
44.207.498.5574 (Fax)

www.silvestertafuro.com

Silvester + Tafuro, Inc.

American Airlines Admirals Club
Newark, New Jersey

Though it represented the third phase of American Airlines' extensive renovation of its terminal, connector and satellite facilities at Newark International Airport, Newark, New Jersey, the handsome new, 6,700-square foot, 140-seat Admirals Club, designed by Silvester + Tafuro, arrived not a moment too soon. Security procedures introduced at Newark and other U.S. airports since September 11, 2001 have encouraged travelers to arrive earlier and stay longer. Not surprisingly, business people flying American Airlines have found its 45 Admirals Clubs to be a welcome refuge from crowds as well as a better way to spend "dwell time." To create a warm, comfortable atmosphere, develop a sense of flow from room to room, and diminish the "railroad car" feeling of the 53-foot by 126-foot space at Newark International, the designers set rooms at 45-degree angles, embraced non-linear forms, highlighted a circular canted wall and ran a skylight along the full length of the club. What do business travelers think of the new Admirals Club? Try finding an empty seat in the three full-service conference rooms, nine individual work stations, reception area, bar area and window-side seating lounge.

Above: View from reception area.

Opposite, lower left: Window-side seating lounge.

Photography: Peter Paige.

Silvester + Tafuro, Inc.

D-Parture Spa
Newark, New Jersey

Charles Lindbergh and Amelia Earhart would have found it all quite amusing. Today's travelers are finding time, money and opportunity in the newest airports to eat, shop and conduct business between flights. How about a haircut and shampoo, massage, manicure or pedicure in a stylish, upscale and calming environment just steps from your gate? It's the latest option, thanks to D-Parture Spa at Terminal C of Newark International Airport, Newark, New Jersey, designed by Silvester+Tafuro Design. Once your attention is captured by the jaunty mahogany, mosaic tile and slate storefront, you enter the compact, 525-square foot store to discover a studio-like setting that surrounds you in an oasis of blond birch wood cabinetry, blond hardwood flooring, suspended glass shelving and Italian glass pendant lighting. Ah... what flight, you say?

Below left: Retail setting for personal care and cosmetics, make-up and shampoo for sale.

Opposite: Storefront.

Photography: Peter Paige.

Silvester + Tafuro, International

Holideck
London, United Kingdom

Left: Entry.
Below: Lounge.
Photography: Keith Perry.

You can meet such interesting people wandering through airports. In fact, research by KLM Ground Services reveals that virtually every category of airline passenger—leisure, family and group travelers as well as business travelers—seeks better airport accommodations. Rather than develop another business-oriented airline club, KLM Ground Services recently enlisted Silvester+Tafuro's London office to transform its futuristic vision of an airport lounge into "Holideck" at Terminal 4 of London's Heathrow International Airport. This gracious, 8,052-square foot space takes the unprecedented step of providing first-class entertainment facilities for both business and leisure class passengers on three levels or "decks," regardless of their tickets or airlines. Besides offering standard business amenities, Holideck proffers such delights as a child-friendly Family Lounge, an Interactive Zone for digital diversions, and the "Haven," where passengers can sink into sleeper chairs to travel wherever their dreams take them.

Silvester + Tafuro, Inc.

Hudson News - Euro Cafe
Chicago, Illinois

Cappuccino with your magazines? Now with periodicals and cafe fare seemingly inseparable, Chicago's Midway Regional Airport cherishes its new Hudson News-Euro Cafe, a co-branded, upscale, 2,568-square foot store, designed by Silvester+Tafuro. Here, a newsstand selling magazines and newspapers from around the world joins a European-style cafe selling pastry, fruit juices and freshly roasted coffee in a delectable blend of cherry wood cabinetry, granite flooring and counter tops and a soffit depicting Chicago's skyline.

Above: Selling floor.
Right: Storefront.
Photography: Peter Paige.

Silvester + Tafuro, International

Sabre
Corporate Offices
London, United Kingdom

Sabre, the leading provider of technology that enables the travel industry and enhances airline/supplier operations, with 2001 revenues of $2.1 billion, has grown so steadily in London that the original, 2,500-square foot fit-out is now a new, 55,000-square foot, three-story office, designed by Silvester + Tafuro's London office. Having worked with Sabre for five years, the design firm presided over the continual expansion of the initial space. However, the new office stems from a thorough review of existing space, a new master plan, and a fresh take on open planning and work station design that should keep Sabre on top of the travel world.

Above: Customer service office space.

Below left: Conference room.

Below right: Building entrance.

Photography: Vaughn E. Ryall.

320

SKB Architecture and Design

1818 N Street NW
Suite 510
Washington DC 20036
202.332.2434
202.328.4547 (Fax)
www.skbarch.com
swilson@skbarch.com

SKB Architecture and Design

SKB Architecture and Design

Fairchild Dornier
Herndon, Virginia

Aviation history was written in 1996 when Fairchild Aircraft of San Antonio, Texas, acquired Dornier Luftfahrt of Oberpfaffenhofen, Germany. Though Fairchild Dornier's birth typifies the aircraft industry's ongoing consolidation, the new company stands out for its incisive strategy in developing the first 32- to 34-seat regional jet and the 728 JET Family, a new line of 55- to 110-seat regional airliners. Fairchild Dornier's new, 48,000-square foot, two-floor office space for 50 employees in Herndon, Virginia has been designed by SKB Architecture and Design as a sales tool reflecting the quality of these products and others. In the elegantly tailored mix of open-plan and private offices, conference rooms and sales center, the spirit of Fairchild Dornier is taking flight.

Above: Open-office area.

Below left: Interconnecting stairway.

Below right: Board room.

Opposite: Reception and interconnecting stairway.

Photography: Michael Moran.

SKB Architecture and Design

Teleglobe International
Network Operations Center
Chantilly, Virginia

Time is money when you're a leading provider of global communications with one of the world's most extensive voice, Internet and data networks. Facing the renovation of a 70,000-square foot, two-story network operations center for 180 employees in Chantilly, Virginia, Teleglobe International, headquartered in nearby Reston, Virginia, retained SKB Architecture and Design to create a suitable new environment as quickly and cost-effectively as possible while maintaining use of the space. Not only has the completion of the network operations center, dining facility and network support facility on the lower floor and operations offices and support areas on the upper floor met Teleglobe's financial and operational goals, it has produced a memorable interior of major spaces linked by a linear public way. With the plasma screen images found throughout the center and various exposed building elements as focal points, the design transforms raised floors, carpet tile, sunflower seed paneling and terrazzo, complemented by mobile furniture, into a dynamic and exciting 24/7 showcase for services aimed at meeting the voice communication and Internet needs of even the most demanding carriers, resellers and large Internet service providers.

Top: Central computer laboratory.

Above: Network operations center.

Right: Marketing conference room.

Opposite: First floor public way.

Photography: Michael Moran.

324

SKB Architecture and Design

Fleishman-Hillard Inc.
Washington, DC

A funny thing happens to some organizations that pursue growth for growth's sake. They strain their resources, neglect clients—and stop growing. Fleishman-Hillard, a 50-plus-year-old public relations agency that is part of the Omnicom Group, grows through meticulous client service in North America, Europe, Asia, Latin America, Australia and South Africa. Just how ably the agency accomplishes this is demonstrated by its newly expanded, 70,000-square foot office in Washington, D.C., designed by SKB Architecture and Design. The project's two phases, spaced four years apart, began with a cultural shift from an open-plan environment to enclosed offices around a formal conference/recreation center, followed by an addition of an informal conference center and other facilities on a new upper floor. The two floors coexist as smoothly as growth and service at Fleishman-Hillard.

Left: Employee recreation area.

Below left: Break area.

Below right: Graphic design studio.

Opposite: Reception and conference area.

Photography: Michael Moran

SKB Architecture and Design   Wilmer Cutler and Pickering
Washington, DC

Out of sight, out of mind. If proximity to power denotes success in most organizations, the reluctance of aspiring leaders to work outside headquarters is easy to understand. Such sentiments were anticipated by Wilmer Cutler and Pickering, a law

firm with an international regulatory, corporate and litigation practice in the United States and Europe, when SKB Architecture and Design conceived a 42,000-square foot, three-level annex for 72 employees of its Washington, D.C. office.

However, the contemporary design has overcome the annex's existing small windows, limited natural light and "bowling alley" footprint through good circulation flow, windows and clerestories that share natural light, and a neutral color palette

spiked with rich accent colors. Now, the annex offices are immediately filled whenever vacancies appear.

Upper left: Cross corridor for future art gallery.

Upper right: Typical secretary station.

Left: Reception area.

Photography: Tom Crane.

Skidmore, Owings & Merrill LLP

2001 K Street, NW
Suite 200
Washington DC 20006
202.367.2600
202.367.2602 (Fax)
somdc@som.com

14 Wall Street
24th Floor
New York, NY 10005
212.298.9300
212.298.9500 (Fax)
somnewyork@som.com
www.som.com

224 South Michigan Avenue
Suite 1000
Chicago, IL 60604
312.554.9090
312.360.4545 (Fax)
somchicago@som.com

One Front Street
Suite 2400
San Francisco, CA 94111
415.981.1555
415.398.3214 (Fax)
somsanfrancisco@som.com

30 Millbank
3rd Floor
London SW1P 4SD
United Kingdom
(0) 20.7798.1000
(0) 20.7798.1100 (Fax)
somlondon@som.com

725 South Figueroa Street
Suite 910
Los Angeles, CA 90017
213.488.9700
213.488.0488 (Fax)
somlosangeles@som.com

18/F Winsome House
73 Wyndham Street
Central
People's Republic of China
011.8522.810.6011
011.8522.810.6056 (Fax)
somil@asiaonline.net

Skidmore, Owings & Merrill LLP

Skidmore, Owings & Merrill LLP

Alcoa
New York, New York

Alcoa's new offices in New York's landmark Lever House building, serve as a global communications hub for over a hundred executives and administrative personnel. The design acknowledges a team-oriented corporate culture by introducing a series of concentric boxes defined by the building perimeter. This perimeter box surrounds the central office box along Park Avenue and the public areas near the core. A central intercommunicating stairway connects the entire office vertically. The space is egalitarian in composition by repeating the same public and private zones on each floor. Public zones contain conference rooms, a reception area, a multi-purpose room equipped to accommodate the board of directors, a tele-video conference room and support areas. The international style 43,370 square foot, five-story office was designed by Skidmore, Owings & Merrill.

Skidmore, Owings & Merrill LLP

Charles Schwab & Company
Investor Center Prototype
New York, New York

The securities industry has not been the same since a young stock broker named Charles Schwab established a discount brokerage under his own name in 1974. So it's no surprise that Schwab is reinventing the business again by transforming Charles Schwab & Company into a "full choice" financial services firm. A visible sign of this transformation can be seen in Schwab's sleek, new, 6,000-square foot Investor Center Prototype in New York, designed by Skidmore, Owings & Merrill. The award-winning design centers on a main lobby or "town square," a flexible space that can host investor seminars, and includes semi-private work stations, private offices and support facilities, all seamlessly blending interior design, brand identity, technology and services. Its fine materials and uncomplicated layout extend a warm welcome to a wide range of Schwab clients, setting the stage for a revolution in financial services.

Left: Approach to main lobby.

Above: Main lobby and web terminals.

Photography: Paul Warchol.

332

Left: PC stations linked to schwab.com and desks for client service specialists in main lobby.

333

Skidmore, Owings & Merrill LLP

Dewey Ballantine
Los Angeles, California

Above: One of two boardrooms.
Upper left: Staff lounge.
Lower left: Reception gallery.
Photography: Matthew Millman.

Heir to one of the most respected names in the law since its founding in 1909, the Los Angeles office of Dewey Ballantine is a fascinating study in how an old-line, New York-based firm has developed a new identity espousing team-based collaboration, centralized support services and office-wide integration. When Dewey developed its new award winning, 50,000-square foot, two-level office, designed by Skidmore, Owings & Merrill for 180 employees, it sought a more open and flexible environment than its previous facility. Its success is displayed throughout the inviting private offices and open work stations, two boardrooms served by a club-like reception lounge, interconnecting stair, video-conference room, case rooms, library, staff lounge and support spaces. Notes Paul Walker, managing partner, "The offices are beautiful, user-friendly in both technology and layout, and convey a sense of style."

Skidmore, Owings & Merrill LLP

CitySpace
Chicago Architectural Foundation
Chicago, Illinois

Architecture has always been played as a contact sport in Chicago, the birthplace of modern American architecture. Why shouldn't visitors to the Windy City stop at the Chicago Architectural Foundation, in the lobby of the historic Santa Fe Building at 224 South Michigan Avenue, before taking one of the many popular architectural tours? Thanks to the Foundation's new, 1,800-square foot CitySpace, an elegant showcase for Chicago's architectural history and newest projects, designed pro-bono by Skidmore, Owings & Merrill, visitors are more plentiful

than ever. What once looked like a retail store now highlights a legendary collection of architectural artifacts in a compact yet spacious-looking setting that concentrates displays in its corners, leaving its center open. CitySpace is filling up.

Above left: Entryway.

Above right: SOM-designed city model and timeline wall.

Right: Media-interactive wall.

Photography: Scott MacDonald/Hedrich-Blessing.

Skidmore, Owings & Merrill LLP

A Financial Services Firm
Executive Floor
New York, New York

How should a 30,000-square foot executive floor be renovated to simultaneously host executive dining and conferences where many participants meet in real time but are not physically present? Such was the design brief a Financial Services Firm in New York recently gave to Skidmore, Owings & Merrill.

The solution, an executive boardroom, management committee room, private dining rooms, open assistant offices and executive restroom, representing an outstanding combination of state-of-the-art technology and modern interior design accented with exquisite Art-Deco era antiques. That

this gracious space only reveals its powerful technology when needed may explain why people praise it so highly.

Above left: Central meeting area.

Above right: Corridor doubling as gallery space.

Right: Multi-media conference room.

Photography: Durston Saylor.

Spector Group

3111 New Hyde Park Road
North Hills, NY 11040
516.365.4240
516.365.3604 (Fax)

architecture@spectorgroup.com
www.spectorgroup.com

12 East 44th Street
New York, NY 10017
212.599.0055
212.599.1043 (Fax)

New York
Long Island
New Jersey
Miami
London

Spector Group

Computer Associates
European Headquarters
London, United Kingdom

Left: One of two intersecting triangular wings.

Below left: Conference rooms facing atrium.

Below right: Virtual enterprise suite for product testing.

Opposite: Main reception atrium.

Photography: Graham Gaunt.

Take a well-educated, highly motivated and intensely creative work force of 920 employees, assign them to a 250,000-square foot, three-story, state-of-the-art office building with naturally lit open-plan offices, meeting areas and enclosed conference rooms, a theater/ auditorium, interior stairways, raised flooring, triangular interior atriums and such amenities as on-site day care, a restaurant, a convenience shop, coffee bars, outdoor recreational facilities and sweeping views of the surrounding countryside— and watch the sparks fly. Such has been the winning formula for Computer Associates, continuing their relationship with Spector

Group, in developing its European headquarters in a suburb of London, United Kingdom, with architecture and interior design by Spector Group and local representation from Blair Associates. Reinforcing the corporate culture of Islandia, New York-based Computer Associates, a $3-billion enterprise software company that provides business-critical technology to over 95 percent of Fortune 500 companies, the new facility gives employees every opportunity to excel in teamwork. Happily, they do just that.

Spector Group North Fork Bank
Corporate Headquarters
Melville, New York

Money center banks are rarely challenged for retail banking customers by institutions from the hinterlands. Yet tradition hasn't stopped North Fork Bank, a mid-sized bank with total assets of approximately $17 billion and 168 branch locations in metropolitan New York, from taking on the big boys. Its feisty, free-thinking, entrepreneurial style stresses relationship building, open communications and easy accessibility, virtues that are celebrated in its 70,000-square foot, four-level headquarters for 250 employees in Melville, New York, designed by Spector Group. Open-plan offices along the windows, private offices clustered in the core, cafeteria, custom-designed, maple veneered furniture and contemporary art suggest why employees value North Fork as much as customers do.

Opposite top: Boardroom.

Left: Chairman's office.

Top right: Executive reception and conference room.

Right: Executive offices and administrative work stations.

Photography: Peter Paige.

Spector Group

Deutsch Inc.
New York, New York

When clients like Almay, Revlon or Tommy Hilfiger visit the cavernous 14th floor of 111 Eighth Avenue, a 2.5 million-square foot, 1930s-era industrial behemoth in New York's Chelsea neighborhood, they know exactly what advertising legend Donny Deutsch, chairman and CEO of Deutsch Inc., a $1.5 billion advertising agency, means by "leaner, meaner, smarter, faster."

The stark, uncompromising, "factory meets art gallery" image of Deutsch's 108,000-square foot office for 455 employees, designed by Spector Group with Fredric Schwartz, comes from using basic materials such as white walls, sliding glass partitions, raw concrete floors and industrial lighting beneath a 14.5-foot high exposed ceiling. With open-plan work stations lining the

periphery, private offices and conference rooms occupying the interior, and street-like corridors traversing the space, the design perfectly embodies chairman Deutsch's insistence on a "no-nonsense, stylish approach" to advertising.

Below left: Conference room.
Right: Reception.
Opposite, upper left: Corridor.
Opposite, upper right: Commons.
Photography: Michael Moran.

Spector Group   Prudential Financial
Executive Headquarters
Newark, New Jersey

Above: Reception area, showing historic displays and statue of "Pru" founder John Fairfield Dryden, outside Dryden Hall, a 600-seat capacity flexible space.

Top right: Dryden Hall.

Below left: Executive area.

Below right: Executive dining room.

Photography: Max Hilaire.

The average American household moves every seven years, but we all know families—and businesses, for that matter—that seem rooted to the land. For example, Prudential Financial, one of the nation's largest financial service institutions and the first to cover working-class policyholders, has resided in Newark, New Jersey since its founding in 1875. Reaffirming deep ties to a city whose ongoing revival is symbolized by the new New Jersey Performing Arts Center, Prudential retained Spector Group to renovate its 582,000-square foot, 12-story headquarters, which houses some 2,500 employees. Consequently, a facility left untouched since 1960 has emerged as Class A space, equipped with state-of-the-art building services. However, the introduction of advanced systems, classic architectural detailing, timeless furnishings and historic artifacts represents more than an upgrade of accommodations. The project positions Prudential for a new era of demutualization that began on December 18, 2001. Now its operations are more visible to the public than ever before, and its people, products and procedures are as user-friendly as possible, a description that not coincidentally fits the gracious renovation as well.

Staffelbach Design Associates Inc

2525 Carlisle
Dallas
Texas 75201.1397
214.747.2511
214.855.5316 (Fax)
www.staffelbach.com
jheinz@staffelbach.com

Staffelbach Design Associates Inc

Staffelbach Design Associates Inc

The Boston Consulting Group
Dallas, Texas

Left: Consultant office.

Below: Support area.

Opposite: Lobby/reception.

Photography: Jon Miller/Hedrich Blessing.

Does anyone's work day only begin at 9:00 a.m. or truly end at 5:00 p.m. in the Information Age? Years before the public debut of the Internet, white collar workers had already begun to notice that their working hours were blurring with their private hours, thanks to the increasing demands of the global economy and the mobility afforded by laptop computers, cellular phones and other high-tech devices. So it was not surprising when The Boston Consulting Group, one of the nation's leading management consultants, asked Staffelbach Designs and Associates to design its new, 26,000- square foot. 96-person Dallas office to operate on a 24/7 schedule. Of course, the facility had to perform tirelessly while providing the consultants and support staff with adequate space and equipment to do their jobs within an environment of timeless grace and dignity. After carefully studying the needs of the workforce at The Boston Consulting Group, Staffelbach Designs and Associates has created an award-winning interior design of private window offices, interior support areas, conference rooms, resource library and break facilities. The facility delivers the required functionality

and physical durability—and accomplishes this in a handsomely appointed setting crafted from such fine materials as Swiss pear wood and maple veneers and limestone flooring, along with fine furnishings. Sensing the uniqueness of the office, Cheryl Gaus, office coordinator for The Boston Consulting Group, observes, "Our primary goal was that it would be timeless. We certainly achieved that goal within a framework of professionals that enhanced the vision we had for the space."

Staffelbach Design Associates Inc

Temerlin McClain
Irving, Texas

Nothing quite prepares visitors for the new, 240,000-square foot office for 670 employees of Temerlin McClain in Irving, Texas. The three-story space wraps around an open, three-story atrium. The design by Staffelbach Designs and Associates marks a significant change in the history of Temerlin McClain. To facilitate the change from a departmental organization to client-based groups, Liener Temerlin, the agency's chairman, and Dennis McClain, its CEO and executive creative director, agreed to exchange a 100 percent enclosed office facility for a 95 percent open plan environment. While Jo Staffelbach Heinz of Staffelbach Designs and Associates conducted the needs assessment and programming process that identified employees' concerns, McClain prepared his colleagues to thrive in a wholly open office environment with few doors and many interconnecting elements. The result, a large yet friendly facility with a clear sense of order. Open ceilings, large, undivided spaces, exposed mechanical systems and applied metal panels surround vibrant neighborhoods and work-based community groupings of open plan work stations defined by "streets" and "walkways" rather than walls and hallways.

Above: Reception view into atrium.

Far left: Atrium.

Left: Stairs, mural and "pulse points."

Opposite: Atrium view into office area.

Photography: Jon Miller/ Hedrich Blessing.

Staffelbach Design Associates Inc

Left: Seating configuration with ceiling modified to raise clearance.

Photography: Bud Shannon Photography.

Air travelers who fly economy class will marvel over a remarkably flexible work environment created in a Boeing 757 aircraft for the Dallas Mavericks, a franchise of the National Basketball Association. The design, by Staffelbach Design Associates, focuses on the size of the players, who include Shawn Bradley, a 7-foot, 6-inch tall center, while complying fully with FAA regulations for flammability, weight and safety.

Ceiling details, for example, are designed to raise the minimal profile to its highest possible point. In addition, this "flying office" features such custom details as premier first class seats that are among the largest in aerospace, meeting tables that quickly convert to cocktail height, side credenzas that open to swallow duffle bags and keep the cabin free of clutter, spacious restrooms for changing, multiple buffet serving counters, and monitors at every seat, multiple movie screens and high-powered sound systems. Sorry—no basket or backboard.

STUDIOS Architecture

1625 M Street, NW
Washington, DC 20036
202.736.5900

99 Green Street
San Francisco, CA 94111
415.398.7575

63, avenue des Champs-Elysées
75008 Paris, France
33 0 44 95 86 60

588 Broadway, Suite 702
New York, NY 10012
212.431.4512

370 S. Doheny Drive, Suite 201
Beverly Hills, CA 90211
310.385.1550

155 Mortlake Road
Richmond TW9 4AW, England
44 208 274 0770

616 Water Street, Suite 317A
Baltimore, MD 21202
410.837.8169

www.studiosarch.com

STUDIOS Architecture

Morgan, Lewis & Bockius LLP
Washington, DC

Right: Law library.

Below left: Reception.

Bottom left: Conference center.

Bottom right: Private atrium office.

Opposite: Solar light pipe at base of atrium.

Photography: Paul Warchol.

Morgan, Lewis & Bockius has a proud history as a Philadelphia law firm founded in 1873 and has become one of America's 10 largest law firms, with over 1,200 lawyers in 16 offices worldwide. Visitors to its new, 320,000-square foot, 14-level, 750-person Washington, DC office, designed by STUDIOS Architecture, may be inspired by more current visions. Suspended in the 12-story high atrium at 1111 Pennsylvania Avenue is a futuristic, reflecting "solar light pipe." Along with an effective space plan that organizes people by practice groups, popular amenities such as a cafeteria and outside deck, and a pragmatic use of materials that balances fine finishes in public areas with basic ones in staff areas, the solar light pipe reveals a law firm that is progressive in serving its clients--and itself.

STUDIOS Architecture

Heller Ehrman White & McAuliffe
Menlo Park, California

Above: Conference room.

Left: Administrative work stations.

Below: Connecting corridor.

Opposite: Reception.

Photography: Sharon Ricsdorph.

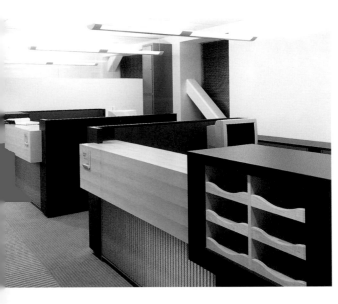

That a creative renovation can be much more than the sum of its original parts is showcased in the recently completed, 85,000-square foot, four-level office of Heller Ehrman White & McAuliffe for 240 employees in Menlo Park, California, designed by STUDIOS Architecture. To develop a highly versatile workplace for this branch of the noted international law firm, the architect enhanced standard office arrangements by negotiating with the building landlord to use the lobby as Heller Ehrman's reception area, using the existing lightwell to distribute natural light on all floors, installing a fitness center, and securing the landlord's approval to excavate a portion of the site to let daylight filter into the basement conference center, dining and food service. The result: an exceptional renovation in more ways than one.

STUDIOS Architecture

Wilson Sonsini Goodrich & Rosati
Palo Alto, California

Wilson Sonsini Goodrich & Rosati, a respected law firm founded in 1961 to represent technology companies at all stages of their growth, as well as the investment banks and venture capital firms that finance them, currently has 600 attorneys working in some 600,000 square feet of offices worldwide. Over the past four decades, the firm has distinguished itself by taking the time to understand its clients' business needs and provide them appropriate legal services. Giving its staff appropriate facilities is also critical. In Palo Alto, STUDIOS Architecture was retained to assemble 290 attorneys and support staff from several locations in a 186,000-square foot, two-level space. To promote effi-cient operations, STUDIOS developed a series of "neighborhoods" linked by circulation paths or "streets," each offering its own complement of attorneys' offices, paralegal areas and library or team workrooms. The color, look and feel of the space has been so favorably received that this design "image" has been replicated in all of their regional offices.

Above: Internal stair.

Right: Cafe.

Opposite: Coffee bar.

Photography: Michael O'Callahan.

STUDIOS Architecture

Paul, Weiss, Rifkind, Wharton & Garrison LLP
New York, New York

Left: Reception.
Below left: Employee dining.
Below center: Hallway.
Below right: Conference room.
Photography: Raimond Koch.

Sometimes the best place to travel is right where you are, as Paul, Weiss, Rifkind, Wharton & Garrison has concluded. The New York office of the full-service, international law firm of some 500 attorneys, ended an extensive site search by undertaking a 350,000-square foot, 11-floor, multi-phase renovation of its existing public areas, including hallways, elevator lobbies, reception areas and conference rooms, with STUDIOS Architecture. Finishes and lighting fixtures were replaced to freshen visual image, the employee dining area servery was enlarged to improve circulation and selections, conference rooms were updated, and a new conference center was built—all without tears or relocation.

The Switzer Group, Inc.

Tower Place
3340 Peachtree Road, NE
Suite 2120
Atlanta, GA 30326
404.842.7850
404.842.7851 (Fax)

535 Fifth Avenue
New York, NY 10017
212.922.1313
212.922.9825 (Fax)

1221 Brickell Avenue
9th Floor
Miami, FL 33131
305.377.8788
305.374.6146 (Fax)

1155 Connecticut Avenue, NW
Suite 300
Washington, DC 20036
202.467.8596
202.429.0388 (Fax)

www.theswitzergroup.com
contactus@theswitzergroup.com

The Switzer Group, Inc.

Pfizer, Inc.
New York, New York

There are no windows in the new, 60,000-square foot training and dining facility on the concourse level of Pfizer's Manhattan headquarters at 150 East 42nd Street, designed by The Switzer Group. Yet everything in this subterranean environment for the pharmaceutical giant (2001 revenues totaled $32.3 billion), seems bathed in sunlight, including an art gallery with a rotating collection, conference center with conference, training and meeting rooms, two private dining rooms, full-service kitchen and servery, 320-seat corporate dining room, and back office area. A sensible floor plan that focuses on the gallery as the hub, a creative palette of durable and light-transmitting materials, including stone, terrazzo, hardwood, stainless steel and glass, and forms and lighting that are both pleasing and functional give the concourse its own, distinct radiance.

The Switzer Group, Inc.

Phillips Van Heusen
New York, New York

If the executive floor at Phillips-Van Heusen Corporation's new Manhattan headquarters is constructed like a well-tailored wardrobe, the resemblance is entirely appropriate. The company, one of the world's leading apparel and footwear makers with such brands as Van Heusen®, Bass®, Geoffrey Beene®, IZOD® and licenses for DKNY®, Kenneth Cole®, Arrow®, and Aigner®, asked The Switzer Group to design its 18,000-square foot executive floor as part of its relocation to 10 floors at 200 Madison Avenue. The floor's eight private window offices, conference suites, administrative staff work spaces, boardroom, pantry facilities and private restrooms are appointed in hand-finished, mahogany-stained cherry paneled walls, oversized

office doors, a vaulted wood ceiling, creme marble floors and classic, traditional-style furnishings that leave no doubt Phillips-Van Heusen is dressed for work.

The Switzer Group, Inc.

MetLife e-Commerce
Jersey City, New Jersey

Constructing something "hip" and "cool" within 135-year-old Metropolitan Life Insurance Company might sound far-fetched until you visit the new, 30,720-square foot, fifth floor MetLife E-Commerce project for 129 employees in Jersey City, New Jersey, designed by The Switzer Group. In this instance, MetLife has deliberately

Above: Reception.

Right: Conference room.

Opposite: Reception furnishings.

Photography: Peter Paige.

sought an energetic, dynamic and interactive facility to foster creativity, teaming and collaborative work. The completed workplace, located atop a building with panoramic views of Manhattan, gives the private and open-plan offices, visitors' offices, team rooms, multi-purpose conference rooms, usability laboratory, cafe, coffee rooms, game room and collaboration room a loft-like, high-technology feeling. The design features work stations with modular work surfaces and low-height vertical panels, and "huts" that enclose office equipment and double as informal meeting places.

Above: Open-plan area.
Left: Private offices.

Ted Moudis Associates

305 East 46th Street
New York, NY 10017
212.308.4000
212.644.8673 (Fax)
tma@tedmoudis.com
www.tedmoudis.com

440 South LaSalle Street
Chicago, IL 60605
312.663.0130
312.663.0138 (Fax)

Ted Moudis Associates

Tiffany & Co.
New York, New York

Below: Executive reception.

Opposite, above: Boardroom.

Opposite, lower right: Gathering area outside private offices.

Opposite, bottom right: Private office.

Photography: Michael Holland Photography.

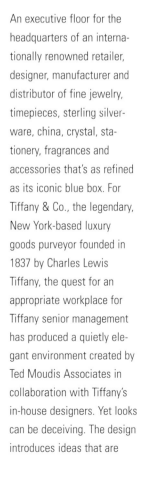

An executive floor for the headquarters of an internationally renowned retailer, designer, manufacturer and distributor of fine jewelry, timepieces, sterling silverware, china, crystal, stationery, fragrances and accessories that's as refined as its iconic blue box. For Tiffany & Co., the legendary, New York-based luxury goods purveyor founded in 1837 by Charles Lewis Tiffany, the quest for an appropriate workplace for Tiffany senior management has produced a quietly elegant environment created by Ted Moudis Associates in collaboration with Tiffany's in-house designers. Yet looks can be deceiving. The design introduces ideas that are more contemporary in spirit than its traditional millwork and furnishings. Each corner of the floor, for example, acts as a private suite and gathering area, while the circulation corridors, conference rooms and drawing rooms double as galleries for original sketches and photography from company archives, providing further opportunities for meetings and interaction. State-of-the-art office technology is also present, of course, presented as discreetly as the revered blue box.

Ted Moudis Associates

Sumitomo Trust & Banking Co. (USA)
Hoboken, New Jersey

Originally established in 1987 in New York as a subsidiary of Sumitomo Trust & Banking Co., Ltd., based in Osaka, Japan, Sumitomo Trust & Banking Co. (U.S.A.) is now a New Jersey state-chartered bank whose deposits are insured by the Federal Deposit Insurance Corporation. An appropriate symbol of Sumitomo's evolving identity is its handsome, new, 37,000-square foot office for 200 employees in Hoboken, New Jersey, designed by Ted Moudis Associates. Situated atop the new Waterfront Corporate Center, the bank's offices supplement plentiful daylight and 360-degree vistas with glass fronts that transmit light and views deep indoors. At the same time, its new furnishings reflect an institution that has been operating in the United States for some 15 years, providing clients with global custody services, securities lending and repurchase transaction services. Fine finishes in neutral colors help assure that the private offices, work stations, conference room, 20-position trading room, data center, archive and file room, vault, pantry and 50-seat lunch-room function as a superior workplace.

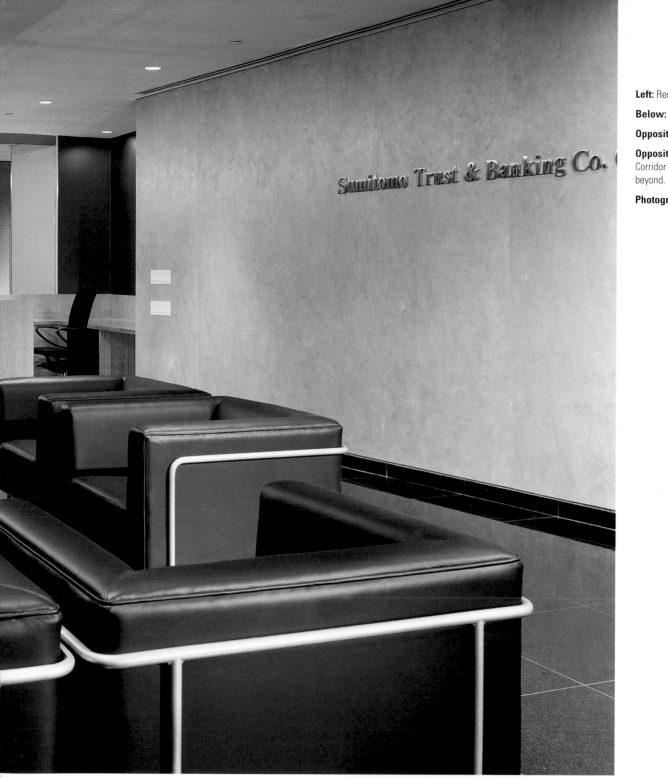

Left: Reception area seating.

Below: Boardroom.

Opposite, left: Elevator lobby.

Opposite, below right: Corridor with lunchroom beyond.

Photography: Paul Warchol.

Sumitomo Trust & Banking Co.

Ted Moudis Associates

Société Générale
Greenwich, Connecticut

Top: Main conference room.

Above left: Traders conference room.

Above right: Trading floor.

Left: Reception area featuring a custom anigre desk.

Photography: Paul Warchol.

Below: Lounge and perimeter offices, featuring anigre millwork, wood flooring and outdoor views visible through glass fronts.

Continuing their on-going relationship, Société Générale, the third largest bank in France, asked Ted Moudis Associates to design their new derivatives trading facility in Greenwich, CT. The design demonstrates the benefits of long-term ties between the bank and its design firm by giving employees a space that simultaneously accommodates and compensates for the fast pace of trading. Admitting natural light and sweeping views of the inlet just off the Long Island Sound, the space offers a sophisticated trading room for 18 positions, complete with custom-designed trading desks, flat screen monitors, pendant-mounted and indirect lighting. Completing the space are executive offices and support space, conference and sitting rooms, and a work-out room. Creating a connection with the surrounding water views, the reception area hosts a custom reception desk depicting a sailing vessel. Considerable attention has gone into the use of materials, with special attention to the architectural woodwork which was carefully selected and matched. In addition to the anigre and maple veneers, the palette of materials include Venetian plaster, cherry wood flooring and leather and velour fabrics, combined to create a warm, inviting work space.

Ted Moudis Associates

Paoli Showroom
New York, New York

Above: Interior view framed by massive column.

Left: Detail of wraparound glass wall.

Below: Product display.

Photography: Paul Warchol.

Architects, interior designers and their clients in the greater New York region who have known Paoli as a furniture manufacturer of traditional office case goods and seating are pleasantly surprised to visit the newly relocated, 8,000-square foot Paoli showroom at New York Design Center in midtown Manhattan, designed by Ted Moudis Associates. The industrial aesthetic of metal and glass enclosed by a wraparound glass wall abounds in such unconventional details as stainless steel industrial floor tiles, massive columns clad in iridescent mosaic tiles, wave-patterned carpet and dramatically recessed track lighting troughs that help conceal portions of the ceiling dropped to house ductwork. So unlike its predecessors in its modernity, this showroom is proving to be the perfect foil for the sleek transitional office furniture Paoli is adding to its line.

VOA Associates

224 South Michigan Avenue
Chicago, IL 60604
312.554.1400
312.554.1412 (Fax)
www.voa.com

VOA Associates

ABN-AMRO Bank
Executive Conference/Dining Facility
Chicago, Illinois

Above left: Break out rotunda with executive conference room entry.

Above right: Conference room.

Opposite: Break out rotunda showing corridor to teleconferencing room.

Photography: Nick Merrick/Hedrich-Blessing.

Doing things right since 1824 may be one reason why Amsterdam-based ABN-AMRO Bank ranks as the 10th largest bank in Europe and 22nd largest in the world, with over 3,400 branches in more than 60 countries, 110,000 employees and total assets (June 2002) of ¤ 607.5 billion. Consider ABN-AMRO's newly completed, 4,800-square foot executive conference/dining facility in Chicago, designed by VOA Associates. Not only does the space satisfy the bank's wish to celebrate the historic Art Deco architecture of its office building, it creates a larger and more versatile executive conference/dining facility than before. VOA's design, featuring a dramatic Art Deco-style rotunda, so skillfully combines custom, 1920s-style furnishings with 21st century technology that the large, pre-function area outside a meeting/entertaining room can use sophisticated movable walls to convert into three smaller spaces that look anything but temporary. Or as George Gershwin would say, 'S Wonderful.

VOA Associates

Ariel Capital Management
Chicago, Illinois

After Wall Street's 200-2001 roller coaster ride, an investment philosophy maintaining "Slow and Steady Wins the Race" may be just what investors need. In fact, it's a winning strategy for Ariel Capital Management, Inc., the nation's largest Black-owned investment management firm, with over $10 billion in assets. When the 65-person firm—whose symbol is a tortoise—recently noved from an open-plan office to one with private offices, it asked VOA Associates to bestow a steady calm to its new, 27,000 square foot space. To achieve this, VOA shaped corridors into meandering pathways that pause at activity zones, installed textured glass to admit abundant daylight, used curvilinear ceiling treatments as connecting motifs, and introduced soft, ambient light from concealed fixtures. Whatever the tortoise and hare are thinking, Mellody Hobson, president of Ariel, declares, "We are simply delighted with the outcome—memorable, functional and uniquely Ariel."

Left: Custom millwork and glass partitions.

Far left: Corridor view towards reception.

VOA Associates

Financial Consulting Firm
Innovation Center
Chicago, Illinois

Above: View through spine.

Left: Main entrance.

Opposite: Atrium space.

Photography: Nick Merrick/Hedrich-Blessing.

So many great enterprises are born to small, determined groups of creative individuals toiling in garages that large organizations may wonder if the global quest for innovation will pass them by. They have cause for optimism. Fortune 500 companies like IBM obtain scores of valuable patents annually.

The challenge for large organizations is to provide enough resources and guidance without imposing too many rules and expectations—and to nurture what will often encounter entrenched resistance. For a Financial Consulting Firm in Chicago, the development of a new, 31,500-square foot,

100-employee, state-of-the-art Innovation Center to foster breakthrough technology, designed by VOA Associates, finds an intriguing equilibrium between forward thinking and corporate values. Like a garage, the Center is built on a minimal budget. Yet like other divisions of the financial consulting firm, the Center shares an existing atrium space in the firm's office building. The award-winning Center deserves attention for its skillful plan and sophisticated looks, both accomplished with modest means. Why does it succeed? First, the Center's circulation "spine" offsets the atrium by leading from the entrance through a majority of the facility. Then, costs are saved through such economies as reusing 50 percent of existing carpet and 85 percent of existing HVAC, lighting and sprinklers, and relying on such staples of interior construction as drywall and paint. Finally, the de Stijl-style design is a tour de force. How better to house an Innovation Center than in innovative design?

Above: Semi-private meeting space.

Right: Carpet patterns reinforce traffic patterns.

WPG Design Group

116 John Street
New York, NY 10038
212.566.5848
212.566.5854 (Fax)
www.wpgdesign.com
maindesk@wpgdesign.com

WPG Design Group

WPG Design Group

Olympic Tower
Lobby Renovation
New York, New York

Right: Main lobby looking south.

Below left: Onassis Cutural Center.

Below right: Concierge desk and elevator lobby.

Opposite: Waterfall with seating area and new skylight.

Photography: Elizabeth Felicella.

Nowhere on the refined curtain wall of brown-tinted glass that soars 620 feet above midtown Manhattan is there a hint of the uniqueness inside the 51-story Olympic Tower, at Fifth Avenue and 50th Street. However, when the skyscraper designed by Skidmore, Owings & Merrill opened in 1976, it was hailed as a pioneer of urban planning with its innovative mix of shops, offices and owner-occupied luxury apartments. WPG Design Group was recently retained to renew the image of the Tower's office building lobby, concierge desk, lobby entrances on 51st and 52nd Streets, public restrooms, retail concourse and imposing, 30-foot high Olympic Place Gallery, a public arcade featuring a signature waterfall and seating area, 15,000 square feet in all. While the original concept endures, the restored waterfall and new security system, dramatic lighting, elegant finishes and handsome furniture assure that Olympic Tower remains one of Manhattan's leading addresses.

WPG Design Group

Can men's clothing be elegant, understated, intelligent and reversible? Known for deftly combining the casual, modern essence of American sportswear with sophisticated colors and fine fabrics, Henry Grethel recently asked WPG Design Group to develop a 4,500-square foot New York studio for eight employees that doubles as a showroom for buyers during the apparel industry's seasonal showings. The resulting loft environment is spacious and inviting, highlighted by interior walls and doors glazed for privacy and daylight, surfaces painted white or finished in natural hardwood, dramatic lighting, and transitional furniture.

Of course, everything defers to the work of Mr. Grethel, a respected designer who created the opening ceremony uniforms for the United States Olympic teams in Albertville and Barcelona. His company likes to say, "Designs make the market and Henry Grethel makes the designs." Here, they make the space as well.

Above: Reception desk and seating.

Right: Conference area for buyers.

Opposite, above: View of studio from reception.

Photography: Roy Wright.

WPG Design Group

Bloomberg L.P.
Plainsboro, New Jersey

Retrofitting a 72,000-square foot, two-story facility in just six months from inception and design to construction—as WPG Design Group has just done for Bloomberg L.P., the global financial information services, news and media company, in its Plainsboro, New Jersey office—is fast track scheduling with a vengeance for the design and construction community. However, time flows quite differently in the financial world, where capital, securities and other assets can circumnavigate the globe in seconds, and downtime measured in minutes or less can end up costing huge sums of money. So when Bloomberg needed to assemble open office areas, training rooms, conference rooms, small meeting rooms, a television studio, an offset printing plant and an employee pantry in the same building, it needed a bold, clear spatial concept that could be swiftly executed while the company maintained uninterrupted operations, and immediately understood and used by the

Above: Second floor data room, stair and first floor data rooms.

Left: Conference rooms.

Opposite: Monumental stair and small meeting rooms.

Photography: Elizabeth Felicella.

390

580 employees upon completion. The new installation is anchored by an interior circulation spine leading from the entrance to the monumental stair, set in a two-story high opening that joins the two floors. The appealing, open environment of the new interior is furnished in a high-tech style which employs a modern architecture of metal, glass, drywall and saturated color to provide the context for state-of-the-art computers, display screens and other information technology equipment and high-performance, ergonomic office furniture. For Bloomberg, an organization with 8,000 people in over 100 offices worldwide that first earned the respect of the financial world by bringing together an unparalleled combination of data, analytics, electronic trading and straight-through processing tools in a single platform, leveling the playing field between buyers and sellers, and has subsequently grown to include global news, television, radio, Internet, and magazine and book publishing operations, the office's restless energy seems particularly apt.

Above: First floor work stations and main ceiling spline.

Right: Training room.

Zimmer Gunsul Frasca Partnership

320 SW Oak Street
Suite 500
Portland, OR 97204
503.224.3860
503.224.2482 (Fax)

515 South Flower Street
Suite 3700
Los Angeles, CA 90071
213.617.1901
213.617.0047 (Fax)

925 Fourth Avenue
Suite 2400
Seattle, WA 98101
206.623.9414
206.623.7868 (Fax)

1800 K Street NW
Suite 200
Washington DC 20006
202.380.3120
202.380.3128 (Fax)

www.zgf.com

Zimmer Gunsul Frasca Partnership

Ray, Quinney & Nebeker
Salt Lake City, Utah

Right: Reception/conference area.

Below left: Conference to reception.

Bottom left: Small conference room.

Photography: Richard Barnes.

After 60 years in one place, Ray, Quinney & Nebeker, a prestigious, 80-attorney law firm in Salt Lake City, Utah, confronted changing market conditions as well as substantial staff additions by developing new accommodations. The firm's recent move to a sleek, 60,000-square foot, 3½-floor facility, designed by Zimmer Gunsul Frasca Partnership to give 150 employees private offices, open work stations, conference center, reception and lunchroom, marked a significant moment in its service to local businesses and the US Olympic Committee. Contemporary style using traditional materials, full-height glass conference room fronts and doors, and internal stairs were some of the ways the design matched the quality of the firm, helped recruit young attorneys, and housed more staff—in record time for the Winter Games.

Left: Primary board room.

Right: Typical attorney's office.

Zimmer Gunsul Frasca Partnership

Safeco
Redmond Campus Expansion
Redmond, Washington

Left: Five hundred-seat cafeteria.

Below left: South Building primary lobby. Artists Paul Marioni and Ann Troutner designed glass floor and walls.

Bottom left: Cafeteria seating.

Bottom right: Gallery from North Building lobby to cafeteria.

Opposite: Ed Carpenter sculpture in North Building primary lobby.

Photography: Nick Merrick/Hedrich-Blessing.

Should financial institutions sell 21st century products from mid-20th-century-style offices? Increasingly, organizations like Safeco want better alternatives. From its founding in 1923, Safeco has evolved into a company selling auto, home, life and business insurance and such financial products as mutual funds, annuities and stock purchase plans through independent insurance agents and financial advisors. In updating its 46-acre

Redmond, Washington campus, the company recently retained Zimmer Gunsul Frasca Partnership to produce a new master plan, two 150,000-square foot, three-story office buildings, the North (Adams) Building for 693 employees and the South (Shasta) Building for 664 employees, plus a new conference center, cafeteria, data center and other campus amenities. Among the fresh concepts ZGF has introduced are a more collegial

environment focused around a central campus green, entirely open offices and gracious lobbies and stairs—a versatile, interactive, 21st-century workplace.

Zimmer Gunsul Frasca Partnership

Zimmer Gunsul Frasca Partnership
Los Angeles, California

Right: Detail of reception area.

Below right: Small conference room.

Below left: Primary reception area.

Photography: Nick Merrick/Hedrich-Blessing.

Honored by the American Institute of Architects with the Architecture Firm Award for sensitivity in shaping the urban environment, Zimmer Gunsul Frasca Partnership recently used the relocation of its Los Angeles office to reaffirm its ideals. The resulting 22,769-square foot, open-plan facility in a down-town high-rise simultaneous-ly enjoys the benefits of environmental responsibility as it fosters creativity and teamwork. For example, all 70 employees occupy mobile work stations featuring maple tops and recycled Homasote panels, gather for staff and client meetings in conference rooms made with recycled newsprint walls and Homasote tack panels, and depend on a lighting system whose motion sensors change lighting levels as needed. Serious stuff—yet playful forms, bright colors and spatial inventiveness also give the office unmis-takable appeal.

Zimmer Gunsul Frasca Partnership

Stoel Rives LLP
Portland, Oregon

The sentiment that there's no place like home recently acquired a personal meaning for Stoel Rives, a leading, 370-attorney, 850 person law firm in the West providing legal counsel to businesses nationwide, when it analyzed alternatives to its existing Portland, Oregon workplace. Guided by Zimmer Gunsul Frasca Partnership, the 450-person office opted to remodel its 170,000-square foot, 10-floor downtown space, and to create an updated image, introduce a state-of-the-art conference center, and develop an "ideal" work station to accommodate attorney/secretary relationships, necessary equipment and changing technology. The project established a primary reception/conference center on one floor, administrative services on another floor, attorneys' offices on eight floors, and core areas reconfigured for greater efficiency on all floors.

Above left: Large conference room.

Above right: Small caucus room.

Below: Main reception/conference center.

Photography: Eckert & Eckert.

Zimmer Gunsul Frasca Partnership

KPMG
Portland, Oregon

Above: Boardroom.

Left: Main reception area.

Below: The Hub.

Photography: Eckert & Eckert.

Smaller private offices, one-size, open-plan work stations, and shared meeting rooms, all designed to support "hoteling," a remodeled cafe and an updated boardroom may not sound like profound changes for an organization. However, for the 200-person Portland, Oregon office of KPMG, these innovations have successfully modernized an existing, older facility. Thanks to a design by Zimmer Gunsul Frasca Partnership, the 40,000-square foot, 2½-floor space now offers an open reception area with spectacular views, efficiently manages the mobile work force, and introduces "The Hub," an intra-office "getaway" where people have needed no encouragement to meet for coffee, casual meetings and work on laptops.

INSPIRE ENVISION ENERGIZE
EXPERIMENT CREATE
ENLIVEN IMAGINE DISCOVER

ENJOY

tim

Meeting Series

Tilt-out, move-away single piece tops make it easy to nest, move and store.

Projects /Sources Index*

ABN-AMRO Bank - Executive Conference/Dining Facility
Design firm: VOA Associates Incorporated

Furniture: Dakota Jackson, Todd Hase
Carpets & Flooring: Bloomsburg
Fabrics: Donghia, HBF, Marvin Feig, Rodolph
Lighting: Baldinger, Kurt Versen, Lightolier, Reggiani
Wallcoverings & Paint: Benjamin Moore, Glant, Pratt and Lambert, Sherwin Williams

Adobe Training Center
Design firm: Gerner Kronick + Valcarcel, Architects, PC

Furniture: Herman Miller, ICF, M2L, Nienkamper
Carpets & Flooring: Prince Street
Fabrics: Vitra
Lighting: Erco
Ceilings: USG
Wallcoverings & Paint: Benjamin Moore
General Contractors: Bovis

Agilera
Design firm: RNL Design

Carpets & Flooring: Atlas, Tarkett
Fabrics: Maharam, Momentum
Lighting: Metalux, Neoray, Portfolio, Tech Lighting, Vista
Ceilings: Armstrong
Wallcoverings & Paint: Maharam, Sherwin Williams

AIG Trading
Design firm: Roger Ferris + Partners

Furniture: Geiger, ICF, Meridian, Steelcase
Carpets & Flooring: Bentley, Forbo, Shaw
Fabrics: DesignTex, Sina Pearson, Unika Vaev
Lighting: CSL, Elliptipar, Zumtobel
Ceilings: Armstrong, Ecophon, USG
Wallcoverings & Paint: Scuffmaster
General Contractors: AP Construction, Standard Builders, StructureTone

Airbus Industrie of North America
Design firm: Mancini-Duffy

Furniture: Brueton, Gunlocke, Harter, Herman Miller, Knoll, Prismatique, Steelcase, Tuohy, Vecta, Wilkkahn
Carpets & Flooring: Durkan, Larsen, Lees
Fabrics: DesignTex, Knoll
Lighting: Elliptipar, Lightolier
Ceilings: USG
Wallcoverings & Paint: Benjamin Moore, DesignTex, Knoll, Novawall
General Contractors: Westport Corporation

Alcoa
Design firm: Skidmore, Owings & Merrill LLP

Furniture: B&B, Gemini, Halcon, Herman Miller
Carpets & Flooring: American Wood Floors, Edward Fields, V'Soske
Fabrics: B&B
Ceilings: Armstrong
General Contractors: StructureTone

Allen, Matkins, Leck, Gamble & Mallory LLP
Design firm: Aref & Associates Design Studio

Furniture: Herman Miller, Knoll
Carpets & Flooring: Bentley
Fabrics: DesignTex, HBF, Knoll
Lighting: Baldinger, Lightolier, Lithonia
Ceilings: Armstrong
Wallcoverings & Paint: Carnegie

American Airlines Admirals Club
Design firm: Silvester Tafuro Design Inc.

Furniture: Chairmasters, Metro
Carpets & Flooring: Bentley
Fabrics: DesignTex, Edelman, Maharam
Lighting: Leucos, Lightolier
Ceilings: Armstrong
Wallcoverings & Paint: Benjamin Moore

Andersen (KPMG)
Design firm: Zimmer Gunsul Frasca Partnership

Furniture: Davis, Geiger, Herman Miller, Keilhauer, Nienkamper
Carpets & Flooring: Shaw
Fabrics: Bellinger, Donghia, Pollack, Sina Pearson
Lighting: Bruck, Tobias Grau
Ceilings: USG

Aref & Associates Office
Design firm: Aref & Associates Design Studio

Furniture: Herman Miller, Knoll, Vitra
Carpets & Flooring: Karastan
Fabrics: Knoll
Lighting: Flos, Leucos, Lightolier, Lithonia
Ceilings: Armstrong
Wallcoverings & Paint: Knoll

Ariel Capital Management
Design firm: VOA Associates Incorporated

Furniture: Aurora, Bernhardt, Dakota Jackson, Geiger, Herman Miller, KI, Knoll, Luminaire, Meridian
Carpets & Flooring: Bentley, Forbo, Nora, Paris Ceramics
Fabrics: Dakota Jackson, Geiger, Knoll, Spinneybeck
Lighting: Cooper, Leucos, Lucifer, Metalux, Neoray, Nulite
Ceilings: Armstrong
Wallcoverings & Paint: Benjamin Moore, Johnsonite, Knoll, Scuffmaster

AT&T Broadband P+D Laboratory
Design firm: RNL Design

Furniture: Herman Miller

AT&T Global Network Operations Center
Design firm: HOK

Furniture: Brayton, Geiger, Steelcase, Vecta, Vitra
Carpets & Flooring: Bentley, Edward Fields, Milliken, Short Stone Sources, Walker & Zanger
Fabrics: Donghia, Knoll
Lighting: Hillman DiBernardo
Ceilings: Armstrong, Decoustics
Wallcoverings & Paint: Benjamin Moore
General Contractors: Turner Interiors

Bain & Company
Design firm: GHK

Furniture: Herman Miller, KI, Knoll, Teknion

Bank of America
Design firm: Nelson

Furniture: Bernhardt, Brayton, Design Link, ICF, INNO, Keilhauer, Knoll, Nucraft, Steelcase, Vecta, Vitra
Carpets & Flooring: Amtico, Armstrong, Azrock, Daltile, Interface, Shaw, Tate
Fabrics: DesignTex, Edelman, Luna, Pollack
Lighting: Elliptipar, Lightolier, National, Zumtobel
Ceilings: Architectural Systems, Armstrong
Wallcoverings & Paint: Benjamin Moore, Innovations, Maharam, Pratt & Lambert, Walltalkers, Wolf Gordon
General Contractors: StructureTone

Barry Bricken
Design firm: Montroy Andersen Design Group Inc.

Furniture: Arnold
Carpets & Flooring: Shaw
Lighting: Kurt Versen
Ceilings: Armstrong
Wallcoverings & Paint: Benjamin Moore

Bay Harbour Management
Design firm: Montroy Andersen Design Group Inc.

Furniture: Jofco, Poltrona Frau
Carpets & Flooring: Bentley
Fabrics: Poltrona Frau
Lighting: Louis Poulsen
Ceilings: Armstrong
Wallcoverings & Paint: Maya Romanoff
General Contractors: Lehr

Beacon Pictures
Design firm: AREA

Furniture: Bernhardt, Herman Miller, Martin Brattrud
Carpets & Flooring: Larsen, Rodeo
Fabrics: Contract Leather, Great Plains, Joseph Noble, Sina Pearson, Zax
Wallcoverings & Paint: Kalwall, MechoShade

Biogen Inc.
Design firm: Sasaki Associates Inc.

Carpets & Flooring: Milliken
Lighting: Metalux
Ceilings: Armstrong
Wallcoverings & Paint: Benjamin Moore

Blattner Brunner
Design firm: Burt, Hill, Kosar, Rittelmann Associates

Furniture: Hag, Herman Miller, Pollack, Steelcase, Teknion, Versteel
Carpets & Flooring: Daltile, Forbo, Shaw
Fabrics: Bretano, Dauphin, Knoll, Maharam
Lighting: Columbia, Juno, Zumtobel
Ceilings: Armstrong
Wallcoverings & Paint: Pittsburgh Paints

An incomplete list of major sources.
For more information please call design firms.

A TABLE IS NEVER *JUST* A TABLE.

OFFICE TABLES INNOVATED AND FABRICATED FOR THE WAYS PEOPLE REALLY USE THEM.

PRISMATIQUE
DESIGNS LTD.

TABLES THAT WORK.

1-888-414-7333

www.prismatique.com

Bloomberg L.P.
Design firm: WPG Design Group

Furniture: Bernhardt, Brayton, ERG, Steelcase, Vecta, Vitra
Carpets & Flooring: Armstrong, Interface
Lighting: Erko, Wila, Zumtobel
Ceilings: USG
Wallcoverings & Paint: Benjamin Moore, Innovations, Wolf Gordon
General Contractors: E.P. Guidi & Sons

BMC Software Inc. Headquarters
Design firm: DMJM Rottet

Furniture: Baker, Bernhardt, Designlink, HBF, ICF, Knoll, Magis, Minotti, Nienkamper, Vitra
Carpets & Flooring: Atlas, Bentley, Constantine, Interface, Prince Street
Fabrics: Bernhardt, DesignTex, Edelman, HBF, Knoll, Maharam, one+one, Unika Vaev
Ceilings: Armstrong, Celotex
Wallcoverings & Paint: Benjamin Moore, DesignTex, Knoll, Maharam, Pratt & Lambert

BMS New Brunswick Cafeteria
Design firm: Francis Cauffman Foley Hoffmann Architects, Ltd.

Furniture: Brayton, KI
Carpets & Flooring: Daltile, Interface
Fabrics: Maharam
Lighting: Lucifer, Metalux, Zumtobel
Ceilings: Armstrong
Wallcoverings & Paint: Maharam, Sherwin Williams

Boston Consulting Group
Design firm: Staffelbach Design Associates Inc.

Furniture: Dallas, Davis, Halcon, Loewenstein, Matteo Grassi, SMED, Vitra, Wilkhahn
Carpets & Flooring: Invision
Lighting: Belfer, Cedric Hartman, Day-Bright, Neotek, Versen
Ceilings: Armstrong
Wallcoverings & Paint: ICI, Koroseal, MechoShade

Boston Stock Exchange
Design firm: CBT Architects

Furniture: Bernhardt, Geiger, HBF, Herman Miller, Keilhauer, Knoll, Lowenstein, OFS
Carpets & Flooring: Armstrong, Interface, Prince Street, Tarkett
Fabrics: Anzea, DesignTex, HBF, Knoll, Luna, Momentum
Ceilings: USG
Wallcoverings & Paint: Benjamin Moore, Sherwin Williams
General Contractors: Payton Construction

Boyce Products
Design firm: Conant Architects

Furniture: Boyce Products
Carpets & Flooring: Cesar Glass
Wallcoverings & Paint: Benjamin Moore, Innovations

Cabot Corporation
Design firm: Sasaki Associates, Inc.

Carpets & Flooring: Crossley, Karastan, Lonseal, Monterey
Lighting: Ardee, DAC, Edison Price, Elliptipar, Ledalite, Lightolier
Ceilings: Decoustics, USG
Wallcoverings & Paint: Devoe, ICI

Cena Restaurant
Design firm: Roger Ferris + Partners

Furniture: Evan, ICF, Geiger, Meridian, SBFI, Steelcase
Carpets & Flooring: Bentley, Forbo, Shaw
Fabrics: DesignTex, Sina Pearson, Unika Vaev
Lighting: CSL, Elliptipar, Zumtobel
Ceilings: Armstrong, Ecophon, USG
Wallcoverings & Paint: Scuffmaster
General Contractors: AP Construction, Standard Builders, StructureTone

CentreGreen One
Design firm: CMSS Architects, P.C.

Furniture: Cabot Wrenn, Hickory, Tella
Carpets & Flooring: Crossville, Daltile, David Allen, Monterey
Lighting: Lite Energy, Old Dominion
Ceilings: USG
Wallcoverings & Paint: Polomyx, Wolf Gordon, Zolatone

Centre Reinsurance
Design firm: CBT Architects

Furniture: B&B Italia, Bernhardt, Brayton, Davis, Herman Miller, Keilhauer, Metro, Wall Goldfinger
Carpets & Flooring: Allstate, , Bizazza, Daltile, Prince Street, VPI
Fabrics: Deepa, Maharam, Spinneybeck
Lighting: Artemide, Neoray
Ceilings: USG
Wallcoverings & Paint: Architex, Benjamin Moore, DesignTex, Maya Romanoff

Centrica
Design firm: IA, Interior Architects

Furniture: Kusch+Co, Wilkhan
Carpets & Flooring: Brinton, Lees
Wallcoverings & Paint: Corian, Formica, MechoShade

Charles Schwab Investor Center Prototype
Design firm: Skidmore Owings & Merrill LLP

Furniture: Gordon International, Keilhauer, Knoll
Carpets & Flooring: Fredda, Lees
Fabrics: Maharam, Spinneybeck
Lighting: Focus Lighting
Ceilings: Armstrong
Wallcoverings & Paint: Benjamin Moore, Maharam

Cingular Wireless
Design firm: Kling

Furniture: Brayton, Datesweiser, Magis, Metro, Moroso, Neinkamper, Poltrona Frau, Steelcase, Vecta, Wilkahn
Carpets & Flooring: Milliken, Monterey
Fabrics: DesignTex, Maharam
Lighting: Flos, Foscarini, Leucos, Lithonia, Louis Poulsen, Targetti USA, Zumtobel
Ceilings: USG

Cisco Systems Technology Center
Design firm: HOK

Furniture: Fritz Hansen, Howe, Knoll, Steelcase, Vitra
Carpets & Flooring: Forbo, Freudenberg, Interface
Fabrics: DesignTex, Kvadrat
Lighting: Ecco, Modular

CitySpace Chicago Architectural Foundation
Design firm: Skidmore, Owings & Merrill LLP

Carpets & Flooring: Metropolitan Tile, Terrazzo
Fabrics: Maharam
Lighting: Belfer, Lightolier, Metalux
Ceilings: USG
Wallcoverings & Paint: Benjamin Moore

Clear Channel Entertainment
Design firm: Gerner Kronick + Valcarcel, Architects, PC

Furniture: Cassina, ICF, Knoll, M2L, Montis, Office Specialty, Poltrona Frau, Porro, Vitra, Zanotta
Carpets & Flooring: Armstrong, Collins & Aikman, Forbo
Fabrics: Angela Brown, Bergamo, Knoll, Larsen, Pollack
Ceilings: Armstrong, Decoustics, Simplex
Wallcoverings & Paint: Benjamin Moore, Duron, Zolatone
General Contractors: Sciame, R.C. Dolner

Computer Associates European Headquarters
Design firm: Spector Group

Carpets & Flooring: Interface

Congress Center
Design firm: OWP/P

Furniture: American Custom Woodworking
Lighting: Winona
Ceilings: American Custom Woodworking

Cotton, Incorporated
Design firm: CMSS Architects, P.C.

Furniture: Right Angles
Carpets & Flooring: Crossville, David Allen, Flor Gres, Mannnington, Masland, Shaw, Summitville, Tarkett
Fabrics: Carnegie
Ceilings: USG
Wallcoverings & Paint: Carnegie, Innovations

Colorado Springs Utilities Headquarters
Design firm: RNL Design

Furniture: Brayton, Davis, Geiger, Krug, Martin Brattrud, Metro, Steelcase, Vecta
Carpets & Flooring: Armstrong, Lees
Fabrics: DesignTex, Knoll
Ceilings: USG
Wallcoverings & Paint: Benjamin Moore, DesignTex

Courtside Athletic Club
Design firm: Orlando Diaz-Azcuy Designs

Furniture: McGuire
Carpets & Flooring: Galleria Floors
Fabrics: Osborne & Little
Lighting: Boyd Lighting
Wallcoverings & Paint: Benjamin Moore

D'Arcy Masius Benton & Bowles, Inc.
Design firm: Gwathmey Siegel & Associates Architects

Furniture: Herman Miller, Knoll
Carpets & Flooring: Lanes, Stark
Fabrics: Cortina Leather
Lighting: Edison Price

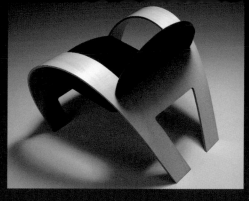

Niilo Chair. Admire it from afar or be admired sitting in it. Forged from laminated wood, it commands a headturning presence. And in spite of its small price, Niilo spares nothing in the way of comfort.
Design: Allan Niilo

nienkämper

Datek World Headquarters
Design firm: Kling

Furniture: Brayton, Metro, Moroso, Steelcase, Teknion, Vecta, Vitra
Carpets & Flooring: Daltile, Milliken
Fabrics: DesignTex
Lighting: Kurt Versen, Legion, Lightolier, Visual Lighting Technologies, Wila, Zumtobel
Ceilings: Armstrong
Wallcoverings & Paint: Baker, Formglas

Deutsch Inc.
Design firm: Spector Group

Carpets & Flooring: Monterey
Lighting: Johnson
Ceilings: Armstrong
Wallcoverings & Paint: Benjamin Moore
General Contractors: StructureTone

Dewey Ballantine
Design firm: Skidmore, Owings & Merrill LLP

Furniture: Bernhardt, Brown Jordan, Cappellini, Donghia, Gerard, HBF, Herman Miller, ICF, Keilhauer, Martin Brattrud, McGuire, Mike, Nessen, Sirmos, Spacesaver
Carpets & Flooring: Constantine, Michelian and Kohlberg
Fabrics: Gretchen Bellinger, Knoll, Maharam, Spinneybeck
Lighting: Artemide, Nessen
Ceilings: Decoustics
Wallcoverings & Paint: Mechoshade, Pallas
General Contractors: Environmental Contracting Co.

DMJM Design Headquarters
Design firm: DMJM Rottet

Furniture: Herman Miller, Knoll, Martin Brattrud
Carpets & Flooring: Bentley, Harbinger, Karastan, Tuva
Fabrics: Edelman
Lighting: CSL, Halo, Liton, Zumtobel
Ceilings: Armstrong
Wallcoverings & Paint: Dazian, Frazee

DMJM Rottet Houston Studio
Design firm: DMJM Rottet

Furniture: Bernhardt, Herman Miller, Knoll, Unifor
Carpets & Flooring: Constantine
Fabrics: Edelman, Spinneybeck
Lighting: Ikea, Kurt Versen
Ceilings: Armstrong

Domus, Inc.
Design firm: Partridge Architects, Inc.

Carpets & Flooring: Azrock, Durkan, Monterey
Fabrics: Teknion
Lighting: Lightolier
Ceilings: Armstrong
Wallcoverings & Paint: Benjamin Moore, Teknion

Dorland Global Communications
Design firm: Partridge Architects, Inc.

Carpets & Flooring: Armstrong, Johnsonite, Monterey, Pirelli Rubber, Shaw
Fabrics: Knoll
Lighting: Lightolier
Ceilings: Armstrong
Wallcoverings & Paint: Benjamin Moore, Knoll, Nevamar, PPG

D-Parture Spa
Design firm: Silvester Tafuro Design Inc.

Furniture: Salon Interiors
Carpets & Flooring: Ardex, Bruce Hardwood Floors
Fabrics: Knoll
Lighting: Color Kinetics, CU Lighting, Lightolier, Zumtobel
Ceilings: Armstrong
Wallcoverings & Paint: Benjamin Moore, Wilsonart

Epstein Becker & Green LLP
Design firm: CBT Architects

Furniture: Baker, Bernardt, Donghia, Geiger, HBF, Keilhauer, Knoll, Steelcase, Teknion, Tuohy, Wall Goldfinger
Carpets & Flooring: Amtico, Armstrong, Atlas, Bentley, Daltile, Fortune Contract, Kentucky Wood Flooring, Lees, Monterey, Stark Carpet, Stone Source
Fabrics: ArcCom, Bergamo, Bernhardt, Donghia, HBF, Knoll, Luna, Maharam, Pollack, Spinneybeck, Unika Vaev, Yoma
Lighting: Alkco, Boyd, Flos, Foscarini, Flos, Les Actuels, Leucos, Lightolier, Sirmos
Ceilings: Armstrong, Ecophon
Wallcoverings & Paint: Benjamin Moore, California Paints, Christa Design, DesignTex, ICI, Innovations, Knoll, Maharam, One + One, Pallas, Sherwin Williams

Ernst & Young Shared Services Location
Design firm: Griswold Heckel & Kelly Associates Inc.

Furniture: Knoll
Carpets & Flooring: Forbo, Prince Street
Ceilings: Armstrong
Wallcoverings & Paint: Benjamin Moore, Pratt & Lambert, Scuffmaster

Equant
Design firm: Heery International

Furniture: Eagan Visual, Geiger, Gordon Int'l, Herman Miller, Meridian, Nevamar, Patrician, Wright Line
Carpets & Flooring: Armstrong, Forbo, Interface, Invision, Milliken, Roppe, SMED
Lighting: Ardee Int'l, ERCO, LBC, Leucos, Lightolier, Lithonia, Visa Lighting
Wallcoverings & Paint: Carnegie, DesignTex, Devoe, Duron, Guard, ICI, Innovations, Koroseal, Maharam, Pittsburgh Paints, Sherwin Williams

Exigen
Design firm: Mancini-Duffy

Furniture: Cappellini, Datesweiser, Herman Miller, ICF, Vecta, Vitra, Wilkkahn
Carpets & Flooring: Interface
Fabrics: Cappellini, Maharam, Unika Vaev
Lighting: IDL Inc., Ledalite, Lightolier, Poulson, Prescolite
Ceilings: Armstrong
Wallcoverings & Paint: Benjamin Moore, Maharam

Fairchild Dornier
Design firm: SKB Architecture & Design

Furniture: Herman Miller, Halcon, Keilhauer
Carpets & Flooring: Durkhan, Terrazzo, Tuva
Fabrics: Deepa, Donghia, Knoll, Pollack
Lighting: DAC, Linear, Lucifer, Schmitz
Ceilings: Armstrong
Wallcoverings & Paint: DesignTex, Maharam, Scuffmaster

Fallon Worldwide
Design firm: Perkins & Will, Inc.

Furniture: Big Design

Financial Services Firm - Executive Floor
Design firm: Skidmore, Owings & Merrill LLP

Carpets & Flooring: Martin Patrick Evan, Jerusalem Gold Stone
Fabrics: Bergamo, Larsen
Lighting: Suttle Cove
Wallcoverings & Paint: Fortuny
General Contractors: Structuretone

Financial Services Firm
Design firm: IA, Interior Architects

Furniture: B&B Italia, Unifor, Vitra
Carpets & Flooring: Constantine, Eurotex, Karastan
Fabrics: Rodgers & Goffigon
Lighting: DFB, Focal Point, Kurt Versen
Wallcoverings & Paint: Benjamin Moore
General Contractors: Structuretone

Fleishman-Hillard, Inc.
Design firm: SKB Architecture & Design

Furniture: Dauphin, DesignLink, HBF, Teknion
Carpets & Flooring: Lees, Monterey
Fabrics: Knoll, Luna, Maharam
Lighting: Artemide, Elliptipar, Reggiani
Ceilings: Armstrong, Novawall
Wallcoverings & Paint: Scuffmaster

Foley Hoag LLP
Design firm: CBT Architects

Furniture: Bernhardt, David Edwards, HBF, Howe, ICF, Kelihauer, KI, Kimball, Knoll, Mateo Grassi, Metro, Nienkamper, Nova Solutions, Office Specialty, Player Chairs
Carpets & Flooring: Armstrong, Atlas, Constantine, Lees, Monterey
Fabrics: Bergamo, Izit Leather, Maharam
Lighting: Color Kinetics, Eureka, Focal Point, Kurt Versen, Lithonia, Poulsen
Ceilings: Armstrong, Ecophon
Wallcoverings & Paint: Benjamin Moore, ICI, Izit Leather, Maharam, Sina Pearson
General Contractors: Turner Interiors

Forrester Research Corporate Headquarters
Design firm: Margulies & Associates

Furniture: Knoll
Carpets & Flooring: Atlas
Fabrics: Knoll
Lighting: Neoray
Ceilings: USG
Wallcoverings & Paint: Benjamin Moore

400 College Road East
Design firm: WPG Design Group

Furniture: Bernhardt, Brayton, ERG, Steelcase, Vecta
Carpets & Flooring: Armstrong, Interface, SMDS
Lighting: Erko, Wila, Zumtobel
Ceilings: USG
Wallcoverings & Paint: Benjamin Moore, Wolf Gordon
General Contractors: E.P. Guidi & Sons

METROPOLITAN, SMALL ARMCHAIRS DESIGNED BY JEFFREY BERNETT.

B&B ITALIA

Fujisawa Healthcare, Inc. - Headquarters
Design firm: OWP/P

Furniture: Geiger, Herman Miller, Knoll
Carpets & Flooring: Forbo, Monterey
Fabrics: Geiger, Knoll
Lighting: Juno, Prisma
Ceilings: Armstrong
Wallcoverings & Paint: DesignTex, Pratt & Lambert
General Contractors: Pepper Construction Company

Future@Work
Design firm: Callison Architecture

Furniture: Brayton, Metro, Vecta
Carpets & Flooring: Armstrong, Bentley, Bergamo
Fabrics: Form+Surfaces, Knoll, Maharam
Lighting: Concealite, ELP, ESI, Focal Point, Lambda, Lithonia, Lucifer, Lutro, Resolute
Wallcoverings & Paint: Benjamin Moore, MechoShade, Scuffmaster

Genry Grethel Showroom and Studio
Design firm: WPG Design Group

Furniture: Brueton
Lighting: Edison Price, Lightolier
Wallcoverings & Paint: Benjamin Moore

Givaudadan Fragrances - Conference
Design firm: Montroy Andersen Design Group Inc.

Furniture: Davis, Keilhauer, OFS
Fabrics: Architex, Carnegie
Lighting: Bruck Lighting, Louis Poulsen

Givaudan Fragrances - Private Office
Design firm: Montroy Andersen Design Group Inc.

Furniture: Dakota Jackson, Davis, Jofco, Source Int'l
Carpets & Flooring: Lonseal, Masland
Fabrics: Carnegie, Maharam

Givaudan Fragrances - Reception
Design firm: Montroy Andersen Design Group Inc.

Furniture: Brayton, Brueton, Dakota Jackson, Harter
Fabrics: Architex, Yoma
Lighting: Louis Poulsen
Ceilings: Armstrong
General Contractors: Lehr Construction

Gray Cary Ware & Freidenrich LLP
Design firm: RMW architecture & interiors

Furniture: Bernhardt, HBF, ICF, Knoll, Keilhauer, Nienkamper
Carpets & Flooring: Interface, Tate
Fabrics: Bernhardt, Deepa, Knoll, Maharam
Lighting: Corelight
Ceilings: Armstrong
Wallcoverings & Paint: ICI Paints

The Heart Hospital at Geisinger Wyoming Valley
Design firm: Francis Cauffman Foley Hoffmann Architects, Ltd.

Furniture: David Edwards, Herman Miller
Carpets & Flooring: Armstrong, Collins & Aikman, Constantine, Permagrain Products
Fabrics: Herman Miller, Knoll, Maharam, Pallas
Lighting: Artemide, Flos
Ceilings: Armstrong, Decoustics
Wallcoverings & Paint: Benjamin Moore

Heller Ehrman
Design firm: Studios Architecture

Furniture: Halcon, Herman Miller, ICF, Knoll, Steelcase, Vitra
Carpets & Flooring: Armstrong, Prince Street
Lighting: Nessen
Ceilings: Armstrong, USG
Wallcoverings & Paint: Benjamin Moore, DesignTex

Heller Ehrman Attorneys
Design firm: Conant Architects

Furniture: Bernhardt, Boyce Products, David Edward, Davis, Howe, Humanscale, ICF Keilhauer, Knoll, Nienkamper
Carpets & Flooring: Azrock, Blue Ridge, Bolyu
Fabrics: Bernhardt, Jim Thompson, Spinneybeck
Lighting: Engineered Lighting Products, Halo, Lightolier
Ceilings: Armstrong
Wallcoverings & Paint: Benjamin Moore

Hewlett Packard Executive Briefing Center
Design firm: RMW architecture & interiors

Fabrics: Carnegie
Lighting: Artemide
Ceilings: Armstrong
Wallcoverings & Paint: Carnegie, ICI

Holideck
Design firm: Silvester Tafuro Design Ltd.

Furniture: Artifort, Johnson, Steelcase, Wilkhahn
Fabrics: Kuadrat
Lighting: Davey, Flos, Foscarini
Ceilings: SAS

Horsley Bridge International
Design firm: Orlando Diaz-Azcuy Designs

Furniture: HBF, Herman Miller, Knoll
Carpets & Flooring: Pacific Crest Mills
Fabrics: Fortuny, HBF
Lighting: Leucos

HQ, formerly Vantas
Design firm: Callison Architecture, Inc.

Furniture: Kimball

Hudson News Euro Cafe
Design firm: Silvester Tafuro Design Ltd.

Furniture: Design Within Reach
Carpets & Flooring: American Olean
Fabrics: Wilsonart
Lighting: BK, George Kovacs, Halo, LBL, Metalux, Tech Lighting
Ceilings: Armstrong
Wallcoverings & Paint: Benjamin Moore

HypoVereinsbank
Design firm: Gerner Kronick + Valcarcel, Architects, PC

Furniture: Acme Architectural Walls, M2L, Office Specialty, Walter P. Sauer, Unifor
Carpets & Flooring: Collins & Aikman
Fabrics: Knoll, Spinneybeck
Lighting: Zumtobel
Ceilings: Armstrong, Simplex
Wallcoverings & Paint: Benjamin Moore
General Contractors: Lehr Construction, Henegan

Ian Schrager Hotels Office Interiors
Design firm: Gwathmey Siegel & Associates

Furniture: Emeco, Herman Miller, Meridian, Unifor
Carpets & Flooring: Ardex, Bloomsburg
Fabrics: Guilford, Kravet, Levolor, MechoShade
Lighting: Alko, Litelab, Luxo, Staff
Ceilings: Armstrong
Wallcoverings & Paint: Benjamin Moore

IBM e-business
Design firm: HOK

Furniture: Knoll
Carpets & Flooring: Dex-O-Tex, Terrazzo
Fabrics: Knoll
Ceilings: USG
Wallcoverings & Paint: Benjamin Moore, Carnegie
General Contractors: Pepper Construction Co.

International Investment Banking Company
Design firm: HOK

Furniture: B&B Italia, Steelcase
Carpets & Flooring: Bentley
Fabrics: B&B
Lighting: Zumtobel
Ceilings: USG
Wallcoverings & Paint: Knoll, Unika Vaev
General Contractors: Environmental

Investment Banking Company
Design firm: SCR Design Organization, Inc.

Furniture: Steelcase
Carpets & Flooring: Bentley, Bloomberg, Interface, Tate
Fabrics: DesignTex, DFB, Maharam
Lighting: Lightolier, National, Neoray, Tech Lighting, Zumtobel
Ceilings: Armstrong, USG
Wallcoverings & Paint: Benjamin Moore, Carnegie, DesignTex, Sherwin Williams, Wolf Gordon
General Contractors: Henegan

iXL Regional Headquarters
Design firm: CMSS Architects, P.C.

Furniture: AGZ, Brayton, Dauphin, Herman Miller, Krug, Martin Brattrud, Steelcase, Teknion
Carpets & Flooring: Amtico, Crossville, Forbo, Shaw, Timbergrass
Fabrics: Architex, Designtex, Maharam
Lighting: Bruck, Day-Brite, LBL, Old Dominion Lighting
Ceilings: USG
Wallcoverings & Paint: Genon, Innovations, Maharam, Zolatone

JPMorgan Private Bank
Design firm: Kling

Furniture: Allsteel, Baker, Councill, Geiger, Haworth, HBF, JPMorgan Collection, Knoll, Rialto, Southwood
Carpets & Flooring: Armstrong, Avalon, Milliken
Lighting: Alkco, Brunschwig & Fils, JPMorgan Collection, Lightolier, Lithonia
Ceilings: Armstrong

For the future of your business

Knoll

Kana Communications
Design firm: The Libman Group

Furniture: Bright, Davis, Herman Miller
Carpets & Flooring: Amtico, Architectural Systems, Bentley, Mannington, Prince Street
Fabrics: Knoll, Luna
Lighting: Artimede, Lightolier, Metalux
Ceilings: USG
Wallcoverings & Paint: Benjamin Moore, Carnegie, DFB, Richter Group, Scuffmaster, Wolf Gordon

Ketchum
Design firm: Burt, Hill, Kosar, Rittelmann Associates

Carpets & Flooring: Ecosources, Forbo, Shaw
Lighting: Alcko, Correlite, George Kovacs, Ledalite, Leucos, Limburg, Lithonia
Ceilings: Armstrong, Simplex
Wallcoverings & Paint: Dupont, ICI, Lanark, Maharam, Metalum, PPG Paints, Sherwin Williams

Kilroy
Design firm: Aref & Associates Design Studio

Furniture: Custo, Halcon, Vitra
Carpets & Flooring: Bentley
Fabrics: HBF, Knoll
Lighting: Eureka, Flos, Lightolier, Lithonia
Ceilings: Armstrong
Wallcoverings & Paint: Carnegie, Knoll

Knight Trading Group, Inc.
Design firm: SCR Design Organization

Furniture: Steelcase
Carpets & Flooring: Bentley
Lighting: Lightolier, Mark Arch. Lighting, Zumtobel
Ceilings: Alcan, Armstrong
Wallcoverings & Paint: Benjamin Moore, Wolf Gordon
General Contractors: Structuretone

Large Automobile Manufacturer
Design firm: H. Hendy Associates

Furniture: Kimball
Carpets & Flooring: Interface
Lighting: Flos, Lightolier, Wila
Ceilings: Armstrong
Wallcoverings & Paint: ICI, Maharam

LeadersOnline
Design firm: H. Hendy Associates

Furniture: Herman Miller, Teknion, Workplace Interiors
Carpets & Flooring: Shaw
Fabrics: Maharam
Lighting: Eureka, NSI
Ceilings: USG
Wallcoverings & Paint: Zolatone

Lichter
Design firm: AREA

Furniture: Brayton, Dakota Jackson, Martin Brattrud
Carpets & Flooring: Constantine, Lees
Fabrics: Larsen, Sina Pearson

Lois Paul & Partners Headquarters
Design firm: Margulies & Associates

Furniture: Steelcase
Carpets & Flooring: Amtico, Forbo, Mannington, Prince Street
Lighting: DAC, Metalux, Portfolio
Ceilings: Armstrong
Wallcoverings & Paint: DesignTex, ICI

Marconi Medical Systems - Visitor Center
Design firm: McMillan Group

Furniture: Brayton, Design America, Herman Miller, Taylor
Carpets & Flooring: Durkan, Harbinger, Karastan, Nora

Fabrics: Guilford of Maine, Spinneybeck
Lighting: ETC, Tech Lighting
Ceilings: Armstrong
Wallcoverings & Paint: Benjamin Moore, Kaduna, Vescom, Wolf Gordon

Madison Dearborn Partners
Design firm: Gary Lee Partners

Furniture: Herman Miller, Knoll, Unifor, Vitra
Carpets & Flooring: American Walnut, Karastan
Fabrics: Great Plains, Larsen, Spinneybeck

Masa's Restaurant
Design firm: Orlando Diaz-Azcuy Designs, Inc.

Carpets & Flooring: Meridien, Pacific Crest Mills
Fabrics: Cowtan & Tout, Frette, HBF
Wallcoverings & Paint: Benjamin Moore

McCarter & English, LLP
Design firm: Partridge Architects, Inc.

Carpets & Flooring: Armstrong, Crossville, Monterey, Stone Source
Lighting: Lightolier
Wallcoverings & Paint: Blumenthal, Duron, Johnsonite, Pionite

Merck & Co., U.S. Human Health Division, Training & Professional Development Center Café
Design firm: Francis Cauffman Foley Hoffmann Architects, Ltd.

Furniture: Brayton, Chairmasters
Carpets & Flooring: Daltile, Mohawk Tile & Marble, Shaw
Fabrics: DesignTex, Maharam
Lighting: Artemide, Contech, Lithonia, Louis Poulsen
Ceilings: Armstrong, Lumasite, USG
Wallcoverings & Paint: Benjamin Moore, Daltile, DesignTex, F&H, Maharam, Scuffmaster
General Contractors: Torcon Construction

Merrill Lynch Campus
Design firm: Kling

Furniture: Bernhardt, Brayton, Bright, Dakota Jackson, Falcon, Gunlocke, Harter, Haworth, Howe, Keilhauer, Knoll, Metro, Steelcase
Carpets & Flooring: Atlas, Azrock, Constantine, Crossville Ceramics, Forbo, Masland, Prince Street
Fabrics: DesignTex, Donghia, Knoll, Larsen, Maharam, Pollack, Spinneybeck
Lighting: Baldinger Bruck, Leucos, Light Control, Lithonia, Luce Plan, RSA, Wila, Zumtobel
Ceilings: Decoustics, Gordon, USG

MetLife E-Commerce
Design firm: Switzer Group, Inc.

Furniture: Bretford, Geiger, Harter, Herman Miller, ICF, Knoll, Martin Brattrud, Metro, Nienkamper, Vecta, Vitra
Carpets & Flooring: Daltile, Durkan, Permagrain, Shaw, Toli, Tuva
Fabrics: DesignTex, Joseph Noble, Knoll
Lighting: Artemide, Elliptipar, Kurt Versen, Leucos, Lightolier, Linear, National, Reggiani, Zumtobel
Ceilings: Armstrong, Ceilings Plus, Tectum
Wallcoverings & Paint: Benjamin Moore, Carnegie, Walltalkers

MLW Aviation and the Dallas Mavericks
Design firm: Staffelbach Design Associates Inc.

Carpets & Flooring: Bloomberg
Fabrics: Momentum, Tapis, Townsend Leather

Morgan Lewis
Design firm: Studios Architecture

Furniture: Dakota Jackson, Geiger, Keilhauer, Minotti, M2L, Nienkamper, Nissan, Vecta, Wilkhahn
Carpets & Flooring: Design Solutions, Masland
Fabrics: Donghia, Great Plains, Pollack
Lighting: Edison Price, Lightolier
Ceilings: Armstrong
Wallcoverings & Paint: Donghia, Duron, Great Plains

Morgan Lewis & Bockius, LLP Conference Center and Vertical Expansion
Design firm: Francis Cauffman Foley Hoffmann Architects, Ltd.

Furniture: Baker, Bernhardt, HBF, Keilhauer
Carpets & Flooring: Constantine, Durkan, Karastan
Lighting: Boyd, Lightolier
Ceilings: USG
Wallcoverings & Paint: Benjamin Moore, Duron, Knoll, Maharam

Morgan Stanley Dean Witter & Co. World Headquarters
Design firm: Gwathmey Siegel & Associates Architects

General Contractors: A.J. Construction Co.

MTV Network Ad Sales
Design firm: Gerner Kronick + Valcarcel, Architects, PC

Furniture: Cappellini, Herman Miller, ICF, Knoll, Steelcase
Carpets & Flooring: Angela Adams, Armstrong, Bentley, Durkan, Expanco Cork, Stonehard
Fabrics: DesignTex, Unika Vaev
Lighting: Edison Price, Elliptipar, Legion, Lightolier, Litecontrol, Zumtobel
Ceilings: Armstrong
Wallcoverings & Paint: Benjamin Moore
General Contractors: Lehr Construction Corp.

Muzak
Design firm: Little Diversified Architectural Consulting

Furniture: Haworth, Herman Miller, Vitra
Carpets & Flooring: Bretin
Lighting: Lithonia
General Contractors: Bovis

NerveWire
Design firm: Bergmeyer Associates, Inc.

Furniture: Furniture Concepts, Herman Miller, Kartell, Knoll, Kron, Lowenstein
Carpets & Flooring: Armstrong, Atlas
Fabrics: Anzea, Blumenthal, Corian, Jhane Barnes, Knoll, Maharam, Sina Pearson, Spinneybeck
Lighting: Halo, Metalumen, Metalux, Translite
Ceilings: Armstrong
Wallcoverings & Paint: Benjamin Moore, Winona

NewView Technologies
Design firm: Mancini-Duffy

Furniture: Herman Miller, Knoll
Lighting: Linear Lighting
Ceilings: USG
Wallcoverings & Paint: Benjamin Moore
General Contractors: StructureTone, Inc.

tella

Formula E | Manfred Petri

NEW YORK (212) 242-8887
WASHINGTON DC (703) 780-9278
TORONTO (416) 752-7750
MONTRÉAL (514) 364-0511

(800) 268-0511
www.tellainc.com

North Fork Bank Corporate Headquarters
Design firm: Spector Group

Furniture: Bernhardt, Cassina, HBF, Metro, Steelcase, Stow Davis, Vecta, Vitra, Wigand
Carpets & Flooring: American Olean, Azrock, Collins & Aikman, Masland
Lighting: Kurt Versen, Louis Pulsen, Nessen, Reggiani, Versailles
Ceilings: Armstrong
Wallcoverings & Paint: Benjamin Moore, DesignTex, Maharam, Wilsonart

Olympic Tower Lobby Renovation
Design firm: WPG Design Group

Furniture: Knoll
Carpets & Flooring: Dakota Jackson
Lighting: Alkco, Edison Price, Elliptipar, Lightolier
Wallcoverings & Paint: Benjamin Moore
General Contractors: Plaza Construction Corp.

O'Melveny & Myers
Design firm: AREA

Furniture: Brayton, Dakota Jackson, Martin Brattrud
Carpets & Flooring: Constantine, Lees
Fabrics: Brayton, Larsen, Sina Pearson, Spinneybeck

One North Dearborn
Design firm: OWP/P

Furniture: Parenti
Lighting: Architectural Details
General Contractors: Clune Construction

Orrick, Herrington, Sutcliffe LLP, Menlo Park Office
Design firm: Callison Architecture, Inc.

Orrick, Herrington, Sutcliffe LLP, Seattle Office
Design firm: Callison Architecture, Inc.

Carpets & Flooring: Constantine, Interface
Ceilings: Armstrong
Wallcoverings & Paint: Benjamin Moore

Oxford Bioscience Partners
Design firm: Margulies & Associates

Furniture: HBF, Jofco, Knoll, Nienkamper
Carpets & Flooring: Masland
Fabrics: Luna
Lighting: Flos, Luceplan
Ceilings: Armstrong
Wallcoverings & Paint: ICI
General Contractors: StructureTone

Pacific Athletic Club
Design firm: Orlando Diaz-Azcuy Design

Furniture: McGuire
Carpets & Flooring: Abbey Carpets
Fabrics: HBF
Lighting: Boyd Lighting

Pacific Sunwear
Design firm: H. Hendy Associates

Furniture: Ark
Carpets & Flooring: Armstrong, Bentley, Interface, Prince Street
Fabrics: Architex, Knoll, Spinneybeck Leathers
Lighting: Leucos, Louis Poulsen, Prudential
Ceilings: USG

Palmer & Dodge LLP
Design firm: CBT Architects

Furniture: B&B Italia, Bernhardt, David Edwards, Designlink, Dune, Herman Miller, ICF, Keilhauer, Pucci, Wall Goldfinger
Carpets & Flooring: Armstrong, Daltile, Masland, Stone Source, Tuva
Fabrics: ArcCom, Architex, Bernhardt, Designtex, Luna, Sina Pearson
Lighting: Alkco, Columbia, Lightolier, Metalux, Zumtobel
Ceilings: Armstrong, Ecophon
Wallcoverings & Paint: Architex, Designtex, ICI, Izit Leather, Knoll, Maharam, One + One, Pallas, Yoma

PanAmSat World Headquarters
Design firm: Roger Ferris + Partners

Furniture: Geiger, ICF, Meridian, Steelcase
Carpets & Flooring: Bentley, Forbo, Shaw
Fabrics: DesignTex, Sina Pearson, Unika Vaev
Lighting: CSL, Elliptipar, Zumtobel
Ceilings: Armstrong, Ecophon, USG
Wallcoverings & Paint: Scuffmaster
General Contractors: AP Construction, Standard Builders, Structuretone

Pantheon Ventures
Design firm: IA, Interior Architects

Furniture: Herman Miller, Keilhauer
Carpets & Flooring: Armstrong, Shaw
Lighting: Artemide, Lightolier, Neoray, Peerless
Wallcoverings & Paint: Benjamin Moore, Carnegie, DesignTex, Knoll

Paoli Showroom
Design firm: Ted Moudis Associates

Furniture: Paoli
Carpets & Flooring: Armstrong, Monterey
Fabrics: Paoli
Lighting: Lightolier, National, Neo-Ray, Zumtobel
Wallcoverings & Paint: Artistic Tile
General Contractors: Builders Group

Para Advisors
Design firm: Montroy Andersen Design Group Inc.

Furniture: HBF, Keilhauer, Lowenstein, Neinkamper, Woodtronics
Carpets & Flooring: Masland
Fabrics: Keilhauer
Lighting: Tango
Wallcoverings & Paint: Maya Romanoff

Paul, Hastings, Janofsky & Walker, LLP
Design firm: DMJM Rottet

Furniture: Bernhardt, Knoll, Martin Brattrud, Nienkamper, Vitra
Carpets & Flooring: Atlas, Fortune
Fabrics: Baumann, Cortina, Edelman, Nancy Corizine, Schumacher, Spinneybeck, Unika Vaev
Ceilings: Armstrong
Wallcoverings & Paint: Benjamin Moore, Jim Thompson, Maharam
General Contractors: Environmental Contracting Corporation

Paul Weiss
Design firm: Studios Architecture

Furniture: David Edwards, Knoll
Carpets & Flooring: Bentley, Edward Fields
Fabrics: Maharam, Spinneybeck
Lighting: Horton Lees
Ceilings: Armstrong
Wallcoverings & Paint: Benjamin Moore, DesignTex, Maharam

Pepsico Corporate Cafeteria, Conference Center and Reception Space
Design firm: Gwathmey Siegel & Associates Architects

Furniture: Cassina, Knoll
Carpets & Flooring: Terrazzo
Lighting: Baldinger
General Contractors: A.J. Construction

Pfizer Howmedica
Design firm: SCR Design Organization

Furniture: Brayton, CCN
Carpets & Flooring: American Olean, Azrock, Bentley, Walker & Zanger
Fabrics: Maharam
Lighting: Kurt Versen, Legion, Visa
Ceilings: Armstrong
Wallcoverings & Paint: Benjamin Moore, DFB, Wolf Gordon

Pfizer, Inc.
Design firm: Switzer Group, Inc.

Furniture: Bernhardt, Davis, Herman Miller, Nordic Interiors, Wall Goldfinger
Carpets & Flooring: Harbinger, Hokanson, Johnson, Masland, Shaw
Fabrics: Brayton, Edelman, Knoll, Spinneybeck
Lighting: Edison Price, Elliptipar, Reggiani
Ceilings: Melto Metal
Wallcoverings & Paint: Benjamin Moore
General Contractors: Lehr Construction

Phillips-Van Heusen
Design firm: Switzer Group, Inc.

Furniture: Donghia, HBF, Randolph & Hein
Carpets & Flooring: Edward Fields
Fabrics: Edelman Leather
Lighting: Reggiani
Wallcoverings & Paint: Benjamin Moore

Private Corporate Client
Design firm: Heery International

Furniture: Bernhardt, Herman Miller, Knoll, Versteel
Carpets & Flooring: Armstrong, Bentley, Interface, Prince Street
Lighting: Artemide, Halophane, Lightolier, Tech Lighting
Ceilings: USG
Wallcoverings & Paint: Benjamin Moore, Designtex, Devoe, Knoll, Koroseal

Private Residence
Design firm: The Libman Group

Furniture: Knoll, Ralph Lauren
Carpets & Flooring: Edward Fields, Hokanson
Fabrics: Brunschwig & Fils, Edelman, Old World Weavers, Scalamandre
Lighting: Alkco, Elliptipar, Reggiani, RSA
Ceilings: Architectural Systems, USG
Wallcoverings & Paint: Carolyn Ray, Silk Dynasty, Wolf Gordon
General Contractors: LWC Construction

ARTISAN

Guest chairs, stacking chairs and tables.

Now with armless chairs and a caster option for guest chairs.

Prudential Financial Executive Headquarters
Design firm: Spector Group

Furniture: Bernhardt, Geiger, Halcon, Krueger, Kusch, Marin, Metro, Steelcase
Wallcoverings & Paint: MechoShade
General Contractors: StructureTone

Quaker Foods & Beverages Headquarters
Design firm: GHK

Furniture: Geiger, Herman Miller
Carpets & Flooring: Interface
Fabrics: Maharam
Lighting: Lightolier

Ray, Quinney & Nebeker
Design firm: Zimmer Gunsul Frasca Partnership

Furniture: Bernhardt, Geiger, HBF, Keilhauer, Metro, Tuohy
Carpets & Flooring: Bentley, Forbo, Mannington
Lighting: Artemide, Leucos
Wallcoverings & Paint: Formica, Nevamar, Pionite, Wilsonart

Red Bull North America
Design firm: Aref & Associates Design Studio

Furniture: Teknion, Vitra
Carpets & Flooring: Bentley
Fabrics: DesignTex, HBF, Knoll, Maharam
Lighting: Bruck, Eureka, Lightolier, Lithonia
Ceilings: Armstrong
Wallcoverings & Paint: Frazee

Related Management Company
Design firm: Mojo-Stumer Associates, P.C.

Furniture: Knoll
Carpets & Flooring: Daltile, Harbinger, Lees, Stone Source
Fabrics: Knoll
Lighting: Artemide, Lightolier, Mark
Ceilings: Armstrong
Wallcoverings & Paint: Benjamin Moore, Knoll, Maharam, Vicrtex

The Ronald S. Lauder Foundation
Design firm: Gwathmey Siegel & Associates

Carpets & Flooring: Karastan, Nora
Fabrics: Knoll
Lighting: A.J. Pistol
Ceilings: Ceilings Plus
General Contractors: Plaza Construction

Rothchild North America
Design firm: The Libman Group

Furniture: Bernhardt, Councill, Herman Miller, KI, Knoll
Carpets & Flooring: Amtico, Architectural Systems, Bentley, Prince Street
Fabrics: Carnegie, Unika Vaev
Lighting: Alkco, Halo, Legion, Lightolier, Metalux, Neoray, Winona
Ceilings: USG
Wallcoverings & Paint: Benjamin Moore, Carnegie, Knoll, Scuffmaster, Wolf Gordon
General Contractors: LWC Construction

RSA Security
Design firm: Margulies & Associates

Furniture: DRG
Carpets & Flooring: American Olean, Armstrong, Daltile, Durkan, Forbo, Shaw
Fabrics: Luna, Pallas
Lighting: Baldinger, Boyd, Bruck, Davis, Linear, Metalumen
Ceilings: USG
Wallcoverings & Paint: Blumenthal, DesignTex, Innovations, Polomyx, Walltalkers, Zolatone

Sabre Corporate Offices
Design firm: Silvester Tafuro Design Inc.

Furniture: Herman Miller, Wilkhan
Carpets & Flooring: Amtico, Interface, Mannington
Fabrics: Hartley, Kuadrat
Lighting: MEM, Reggiani
Ceilings: SAS
Wallcoverings & Paint: Delux Paints
General Contractors: Brennan Group

Safeco Redmond Campus Expansion
Design firm: Zimmer Gunsul Frasca Partnership

Furniture: Herman Miller
Carpets & Flooring: Collins & Aikman, Lees, Masland
Fabrics: Herman Miller, Spinneybeck, Unika Vaev
Lighting: Lincar
Ceilings: USG
Wallcoverings & Paint: Benjamin Moore, ICI, Knoll, Pittsburgh Paints

Sandler O'Neill & Partners LP
Design firm: SCR Design Organization

Furniture: Keilhauer, Knoll
Carpets & Flooring: Bentley
Fabrics: Keilhauer
Lighting: Mark
Ceilings: Armstrong
Wallcoverings & Paint: Benjamin Moore

San Francisco Giants Corporate Offices
Design firm: Callison Architecture, Inc.

Furniture: Bernhardt, Davis, Keilhauer, Knoll, Thonet
Carpets & Flooring: Bentley, Interface
Fabrics: Donghia, Knoll, Rogers and Goffigon, Sina Pearson
Lighting: Candela, Denise Forg
Ceilings: Armstrong
Wallcoverings & Paint: Carnegie, Maharam

Sauer-Danfoss, Inc. - Executive Office
Design firm: OWP/P

Furniture: Herman Miller, Knoll, Steelcase
Carpets & Flooring: Constantine
Lighting: Focal Point, Leucos, Lightolier, Tango
Ceilings: USG
Wallcoverings & Paint: Benjamin Moore, Carnegie, Maharam

Schinnerer Group, Inc. Headquarters
Design firm: RTKL

Furniture: Bright, Haworth
Carpets & Flooring: Constantine
Fabrics: HBF, Jim Thompson
Ceilings: Armstrong
Wallcoverings & Paint: Benjamin Moore, Knoll

Sempra Energy Trading Expansion
Design firm: Roger Ferris + Partners

Furniture: Evan, Geiger, ICF, Meridian, SBFI, Steelcase
Carpets & Flooring: Bentley, Forbo, Shaw
Fabrics: DesignTex, Sina Pearson, Unika Vaev
Lighting: CSL, Elliptipar, Zumtobel
Ceilings: Armstrong, Ecophon, USG
Wallcoverings & Paint: Scuffmaster
General Contractors: AP Construction, Standard Builders, StructureTone

Seyfarth Shaw
Design firm: Sasaki Associates Inc.

Carpets & Flooring: Constantine
Lighting: Edison Price, Ledalite, Leucos, Lightolier, Tech Lighting, Zumtobel
Ceilings: Armstrong
Wallcoverings & Paint: Benjamin Moore, Nass Fresco Finishes
General Contractors: Turner Interiors

Shinsei Bank
Design firm: RTKL

Furniture: Bernhardt, Geiger, Herman Miller
Carpets & Flooring: Bentley, Interface, Lees, Shaw
Fabrics: ABF Textiles, ArcCom, Architex, DesignTex, Pollack

Showcase for Building Environments - Brengel Technology Center
Design firm: McMillan Group

Furniture: Bernhardt, CCN, Herman Miller, Metro, Taylor, Vecta
Carpets & Flooring: Lees, Lonseal
Fabrics: Guilford of Maine, MDC
Lighting: ETC, LSI, Tech Lighting
Ceilings: Armstrong, Radican
Wallcoverings & Paint: Benjamin Moore, Lumasite, Zolatone

Sillerman Company
Design firm: Gerner Kronick + Valcarcel, Architects, PC

Furniture: Acme Architectural Walls, M2L, Unifor, Walter P. Sauer
Carpets & Flooring: Magnon Terrazzo, Prince Street
Lighting: Zumtobel
Ceilings: Armstrong, Decoustics
Wallcoverings & Paint: Benjamin Moore
General Contractors: AJ Contracting

Societe Generale
Design firm: Ted Moudis Associates

Furniture: Empire, Fabrizi
Fabrics: DFB
General Contractors: Pavarini

Southern Polytechnic State University School of Architecture
Design firm: Heery International

Furniture: Faxton Patterson, Gordon Int'l, Howe, ICF, Keilhauer, Neinkamper, SMED, Steelcase, Thonet, Vecta, Vitra, Wabash
Carpets & Flooring: Armstrong, Daltile, Forbo, Shaw
Lighting: Lithonia
Ceilings: USG
Wallcoverings & Paint: Benjamin Moore, ICI

GEIGER

Settings™

fits in. stands out.

Spang & Company
Design firm: Burt, Hill, Kosar, Rittelmann Associates

Furniture: Brayton, Herman Miller
Carpets & Flooring: Collins & Aikman
Lighting: Lithonia, Tech Lighting
Ceilings: Armstrong
Wallcoverings & Paint: Sherwin Williams

SRAM Headquarters
Design firm: RTKL

Furniture: Steelcase
Carpets & Flooring: Mannington
Fabrics: Architex, DesignTex, Unika Vaev
Lighting: Lightolier, Lytespan, Metalux
Wallcoverings & Paint: Benjamin Moore, DesignTex
General Contractors: Turner Interiors

Steedman Wilson
Design firm: Little Diversified Architectural Consulting

Furniture: Steelcase
Carpets & Flooring: Prince Street
Fabrics: Architex, DesignTex, One + One
Lighting: Cooper Lighting, Lightolier
Wallcoverings & Paint: Dupon Paint
General Contractors: Westport

Stoel Rives LLP
Design firm: Zimmer Gunsul Frasca Partnership

Furniture: Bernhardt, Howe, Keilhauer, Knoll, Martin Brattrud, Nienkamper
Carpets & Flooring: Armstrong, Forbo, Shaw
Fabrics: Bernhardt, Knoll, Spinneybeck
Lighting: Elliptipar, Zumtobel
Wallcoverings & Paint: Maharam

SubZero Contractors
Design firm: H. Hendy Associates

Furniture: Brayton, Herman Miller, Tangram Studio
Fabrics: APG Tile
Lighting: Lightolier

Subaru of America - Operations Headquarters
Design firm: Nelson

Furniture: Steelcase
Carpets & Flooring: American Olean, Milliken
Fabrics: DesignTex, Knoll, Maharam
Lighting: Ledalite, Lightolier
Ceilings: USG

Sumitomo Trust & Banking Co. (USA)
Design firm: Ted Moudis Associates

Furniture: Haworth
Carpets & Flooring: Constantine
Lighting: Zumtobel
Wallcoverings & Paint: Anya Larkin

Teleglobe International Network Operations Centers
Design firm: SKB Architecture & Design

Furniture: Herman Miller, Keilhauer, Knoff, Touhy
Carpets & Flooring: Constantine, Durkan, Prince Street, Terrazzo
Fabrics: Knoll, Luna, Unika Vaev
Lighting: Louis Poulsen, Zumtobel
Ceilings: Armstrong
Wallcoverings & Paint: Innovations, Scuffmaster
General Contractors: Turner Interiors

Tellabs
Design firm: OWP/P

Furniture: Knoll
Carpets & Flooring: Mannington
Fabrics: Knoll, Spinneybeck
Lighting: ETC, Eureka, Kurt Versen, Lithonia, Lucifer, Rambusch, Tech Lighting, Zumtobel
Ceilings: Armstrong, USG
Wallcoverings & Paint: Benjamin Moore, Knoll, Maharam
General Contractors: Pepper Construction Company

Tiffany & Co.
Design firm: Ted Moudis Associates

Furniture: Baker, Bernhardt, Bright, Brueton, Cabot Wrenn, Councill, Girsberger, Haworth, HBF, J. Robert Scott, Knoll, Ralph Lauren, Saladino
Carpets & Flooring: Atlas, DesignWeave, Eaton, Monterey
Fabrics: Arccom, Duross, Henry Calvin, Jim Thompson, Pollack, Robert Allen, Rubelli
Lighting: Edison, Hinson, HRS, Reggiani, Zumtobel
Wallcoverings & Paint: Benjamin Moore, Blumenthal, Cowtan & Tout, Donghia, Maharam

Timerlin McClain
Design firm: Staffelbach Design Associates Inc.

Furniture: Brayton, Herman Miller, ICF, Knoll, Steelcase, Wilkhahn
Carpets & Flooring: Constantine
Lighting: Artemide, Lightolier, Zumtobel
Ceilings: Armstrong
Wallcoverings & Paint: DesignTex, Polomyx

TJX Companies Headquarters
Design firm: Sasaki Associates Inc.

Furniture: Allermuir, Design Link, Thonet
Carpets & Flooring: Eco Stone, Interface
Lighting: Belfer, Estiluz, Foscarini, Legion, Litelab, Linear Lighting, Louis Poulsen
Ceilings: Armstrong
Wallcoverings & Paint: Benjamin Moore, Duron, Scuffmaster, Zolatone
General Contractors: Payton Construction

T-Mobile
Design firm: Conant Architects

Furniture: Design Resource Group, Design within Reach, Gordon International, HON, Knoll, Office Furniture Heaven, Patrician
Carpets & Flooring: Armstrong, Eco Surfaces, Flexco, Mannington
Fabrics: Maharam, Unika Vaev
Lighting: Ledalite, Legion, Lightolier, Mercury, Metalux, Tech Lighting
Ceilings: Armstrong, Tectum, USG
Wallcoverings & Paint: Benjamin Moore, Maharam

Tribune Interactive
Design firm: Perkins & Will, Inc.

Furniture: Herman Miller, Keilhauer, Knoll, Meridian, SMED, Vitra
Carpets & Flooring: Bentley, Collins & Aikman
Lighting: ETC, Focal Point, Juno, Lightolier, Louis Poulsen
Ceilings: USG
Wallcoverings & Paint: Sherwin Williams

Turner Entertainment
Design firm: Perkins & Will, Inc.

Furniture: Brayton, Herman Miller, ICF, Knoll
Carpets & Flooring: Bentley, Forbo, Shaw, U.S. Mosaic Tile
Fabrics: DesignTex, HBF, Knoll
Lighting: Cooper, Equinox, Metalux, Zumtobel
Ceilings: USG
Wallcoverings & Paint: Sherwin Williams, Wall Talker
General Contractors: Turner Interiors

Turnstone e-Commerce Store and Showroom
Design firm: Little Diversified Architectural Consulting

Furniture: Turnstone
Carpets & Flooring: Milliken
Fabrics: Architex, DesignTex, One + One
Lighting: George Kovacs, Tech Lighting
Wallcoverings & Paint: Duron
General Contractors: Pepper Construction

UBS Paine Webber
Design firm: Heery International

Furniture: Baker, Cabot Wrenn, Councill, Gunlocke, HBF, Kimball, Nevers, NuCraft, Steelcase, Vecta
Carpets & Flooring: Armstrong, DesignWeave, Kentucky Wood Flooring, Mannington, Roppe
Fabrics: ArcCom, Brayton, Designtex, Kravet
Lighting: Alko, Baldinger, Davis/Muller, Kurt Versen, USA Illumination, Zumtobel
Ceilings: Celotex
Wallcoverings & Paint: Benjamin Moore, Devor, Duron, Eurotex Wall Carpet, Koroseal, Sherwin Williams, Vicrtex
General Contractors: Hitt Construction

Vivendi Universal Games
Design firm: Aref & Associates Design Studio

Furniture: Halcon, HBF, Herman Miller, ICF, Knoll, Vitra
Carpets & Flooring: Karastan
Fabrics: DesignTex, Knoll, Maharam
Lighting: Artemide, Eureka, Leucos, Lightolier, Louis Poulsen, Zumtobel
Ceilings: Armstrong
Wallcoverings & Paint: Carnegie, Frazee
General Contractors: Environmental Contracting Corporation

Vocus, Inc.
Design firm: GHK

Furniture: Brylee, Geiger, Indiana Desk, Johnson, Lowenstein, National, Nevamar, Versteel
Carpets & Flooring: Mannington, Patcraft Carpet
Fabrics: Maharam
Lighting: Lightolier, Stonco
Ceilings: Armstrong
Wallcoverings & Paint: Lamin-Art, Sherwin Williams, Wilsonart

Wachovia Corporation
Design firm: Nelson

Furniture: Baker, HBF, Wilkhahn
Carpets & Flooring: Amtico, Bolyu, Glen Eden
Fabrics: DesignTex, HBF
Lighting: Boyd, Lightolier, Metalumen, Winona
Ceilings: Armstrong, Eurospan
Wallcoverings & Paint: DesignTex, Jim Thompson, Koraseal, Thompson

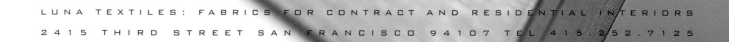
LUNA TEXTILES: FABRICS FOR CONTRACT AND RESIDENTIAL INTERIORS
2415 THIRD STREET SAN FRANCISCO 94107 TEL 415.252.7125

Weil, Gotshal & Manges
Design firm: Mancini-Duffy

Furniture: Brayton, Datesweiser, Gunlocke, Herman Miller, Howe, Inscape, Knoll, Leland, Tuohy
Carpets & Flooring: Constantine
Fabrics: ArcCom, Architex, Carnegie, DesignTex, Luna, Maharam
Lighting: Lightolier, Zumtobel
Ceilings: Ecophon, USG
Wallcoverings & Paint: Benjamin Moore, Novawall, Stone Source

We're Group
Design firm: Mojo-Stumer Associates, P.C.

Carpets & Flooring: Daltile, Karastan
Fabrics: Silk & Contract Fabrics Inc.
Lighting: PSM Lighting
Wallcoverings & Paint: Benjamin Moore

Wharton School of Business, Wharton West Center
Design firm: RMW architecture & interiors

Furniture: Bernhardt, David Edwards, Geiger, Knoll, Stylex, Thonet, Vitra
Carpets & Flooring: Armstrong, Atlas, Dupont, Permagrain
Fabrics: Maharam
Lighting: Cooper, Erco, Kurt Versen, Peerless, Zumtobel
Ceilings: Armstrong
Wallcoverings & Paint: Benjamin Moore, Carnegie, ICI, Knoll, Maharam, Sherwin Williams

Wilmer Cutler & Pickering
Design firm: SKB Architecture & Design

Furniture: Bernhardt, HBF
Carpets & Flooring: Constantine, Stone Source, Walker Zanger
Fabrics: Carnegie, Donghia, HBF, Knoll, Pallas
Lighting: ITC, Leucos, Regianni, Zumtobel
Ceilings: Armstrong, Novawall
Wallcoverings & Paint: Architectural Coatings, Knoll, Pallas

Wilson Sonsini
Design firm: Studios Architecture

Furniture: Keilhauer, Knoll
Carpets & Flooring: Azrock, Bentley, Prince Street
Lighting: Focal Point
Ceilings: Armstrong
Wallcoverings & Paint: Benjamin Moore

Winston & Strawn
Design firm: Gary Lee Partners

Furniture: Bright
Carpets & Flooring: Monterrey, Wilsonart
Lighting: Colombia, Kurt Versen
Ceilings: USG
Wallcoverings & Paint: Pratt & Lambert

Workshop 2010
Design firm: RNL Design

Furniture: Steelcase
Carpets & Flooring: Milliken
Fabrics: DesignTex
Lighting: Lightolier

Xplorion
Design firm: Burt, Hill, Kosar, Rittelmann Associates

Carpets & Flooring: Bruce, DesignWeave
Lighting: Concealite, Iris, Lithonia, Tech Lighting
Wallcoverings & Paint: Benjamin Moore, Zolatone

Yahoo!
Design firm: RMW architecture & interiors

Furniture: Design America, Keilhauer, Teknion
Carpets & Flooring: Shaw
Fabrics: Architex, Deepa, Donghia, Luna, Maharan, Unika Vaev
Lighting: Boyd, Shaper
Ceilings: Armstrong, USG
Wallcoverings & Paint: Carnegie, ICI Paints

Young Conaway Stargatt & Taylor, LLP
Design firm: Francis Cauffman Foley Hoffmann Architects, Ltd.

Furniture: Baker, Bernhardt, Brayton
Carpets & Flooring: Prince Street
Fabrics: Maharam, Novamall
Lighting: Boyd, RSA Lighting
Ceilings: Armstrong
Wallcoverings & Paint: Benjamin Moore, Novawall

Zimmer Gunsul Frasca Partnership Los Angeles Office
Design firm: Zimmer Gunsul Frasca Partnership

Furniture: Heller, Herman Miller, HON, Metro, Vitra
Carpets & Flooring: Armstrong, Masland
Lighting: Louis Poulsen, Zumtobel
Wallcoverings & Paint: Nevamari

Less
designed by
Jean Nouvel

Naos System
designed by
Studio Cerri &
Associati

Progetto 25
designed by
Luca Meda

Unifor
149 Fifth Avenue
New York, NY 10010

Tel: 212.673.3434
Fax: 212.673.7317
unifor@uniforusa.com

RIDE™ *to work*
and shift into gear

The Ride™ seating series represents a new benchmark in high-performance task seating. Its unique multi-function technology enables arm-height, arm-pivot and lock, arm-width and arm-depth adjustments with a single action. Shift levers at the side of the seat control the synchro-tilt mechanism and seat height with unprecedented ease. Back options include dimensional mesh (shown), upholstered and non-upholstered contoured plastic, as well as fully-upholstered styles with adjustable lumbar support. Contact your Global dealer or sales representative for a test Ride™— and a price that you have come to expect only from Global.

 GLOBAL 560 Supertest Road Downsview Ontario Canada M3J 2M6 Tel (416) 661-3660 Visit us on the web at GlobalTotalOffice.com

Medallions

Architex Homage Collection:
Imaginative textile interpretations of people, places, and things.

SULLIVAN CHICAGO
Architex®

SULLIVAN
COLLECTION

architex-ljh.com
800.621.0827

Chair: Poema by Cabot Wrenn
an Architex furniture partner

B O Y D

Somewhere, someplace you've experienced a MechoShade® hard at work.

It could have been at the office, school, auditorium, hospital or someone's home that you experienced the beauty and functionality of a MechoShade®. Now, more than ever, MechoShade roller shades are being specified for their esthetic and functional design characteristics of visibility, solar protection and low maintenance for homes, offices and corporate spaces. Available in manual, motorized or computerized solar tracking systems, visibly transparent MechoShades are the ideal solar protection solution for typical windows, skylights, greenhouses or atriums where greater use of natural daylight is desired. MechoShade roller shades are also available as room darkening shades or blackout for audio/visual integration and/or privacy.

MechoShade features ThermoVeil®, EuroVeil™ and Soleil™ shade cloths which are available in a broad range of colors, textures weaves and densities which meet or exceed the demands of the most discriminating designer and compliment all types of glazing from clear to reflective.

For more information contact your local MechoShade representative by calling Toll Free 1-877-774-2572 or at our website at http://www.mechoshade.com

MechoShade Systems, Inc. • 42-03 35th Street, Long Island City, NY 11101

DONGHIA® STUDIO

DONGHIA'S SIGNATURE STYLE NOW AVAILABLE FOR TODAY'S CONTRACT MARKET.

C O L O R™

Relaxed Khaki {SW 6149}

ANNOUNCING A COMPLETELY NEW WAY TO LOOK AT COLOR.

The New Sherwin-Williams COLOR System has more than 1,000 original colors and new tools to help you specify them.

See your Sherwin-Williams Architectural Account Executive or call 800-524-5979 to have a representative contact you.

The Colors. The Paint. The Possibilities.™

www.sherwin-williams.com

Ultron®: color + performance

Ultron®: unequalled lovely lifetime warranty

Ultron®: possiblities

Ultron®: unparalleled beautifully branded nylon 6,6 carpet fiber

Ultron®: adventure

{ Ultron® is a Solutia registered trademark for its premium nylon 6,6 carpet fiber. © 2003 Solutia Inc. Artwork © Cornel Rubino. }

THE FINE ARTS BLDG.

The Home of the Finest Quality Resources

232 East 59th Street, New York, NY 10022   Telephone: (212) 759-6935 • Fax: (212) 758-7598

345 CALIFORNIA • AWAHNEE HOTEL • AAMES FINANCIAL • ABBOTT LABORATORIES • ACCLAIM ENTERTAINMENT • AIG PROPERTIES • AIR JAMAICA • AIR SHAMROCK • AL BATEEN PALACE • ALABAMA FARMERS FEDERATION • ALAN JACKSON MUSEUM • ALAINT BANK • ALLIANCE CAPITAL • ALLSTEEL, INC. • ALLTEL SERVICE CORPORATION • AMERICAN AIRLINES • AMERICAN BROADCASTING COMPANY • AMERICAN EXPRESS • AMERICAN MUTUAL INSURANCE • AMERITECH • AMSTED INDUSTRIES • ANSETT AIR • ARAMCO • ARKANSAS CANCER RESEARCH • AT&T • ARNOLD & PORTER • ARTHUR ANDERSON • AUTO ONE • BANCO MERCANTILE • BANPAIS • BARGER & MOSS • BARON CAPITAL BAXTER • BEAU RIVAGE • BECTON DICKINSON • BELAGIO HOTEL • BERTLESMAN • BLUE CROSS BLUE SHIELD • BOEING COMMERCIAL AIRPLANE CO. • BOEING EXECUTIVE LOBBY • BRADLEY, ARANT, ROSE & WHITE • BRISTOL MEYERS • CANTOR FITZGERALD • CAPITAL GROUP • CAPITAL RECORDS • CARTER WALLACE • CHAPMAN EXPLORATION • CHASE BANK OF TEXAS, N.A. • CHASE MANHATTAN BANK • CHEMICAL BANK • CHICAGO MERCANTILE EXCHANGE • CHURCH OF THE NATIVITY, EPISCOPAL CHURCH • CITIBANK • CITIBANK MEADOW BANK GOVERNMENT CENTER • CITICORP • CITIFLIGHT • CLAYTON CENTER • COCA COLA • COLE-HAAN • COWEN & CO. • CREDIT SUISSE • COMMERZBANK • CROWN PRINCESS • CUSHMAN & WAKEFIELD • DALLAS CONVENTION CENTER • DALLAS COUNTRY CLUB • DALLAS MUSEUM OF ART • DAVIS POLK WARDWELL • DAWN PRINCESS • DEAN WITTER • DEAN WITTER DRAGORO • DEL WEBB CORPORATION • DEWEY BALLANTINE • DIME SAVINGS BANK • DOCTOR'S CENTER • DOMINO'S PIZZA • DRAGOCO • DUKE ENERGY • E.A.J. CORPORATION • EASTMAN KODAK • ELEVEN HUNDRED UNION PACIFIC • ELI LILY • ENPRO INTERNATIONAL • ENSAFE • EQUITABLE LIFE • EQUITY OFFICE PROPERTIES • ESSENCE COMMUNICATIONS • ETHIOPIAN AIRLINES • EXXON • F & M BANK • FAISON STONE • FANNIE MAE FOUNDATION • FEDERAL RESERVE BANK OF NEW YORK • FIRST BANK • FIDUCIARY TRUST • FIRST CHICAGO BANK • FIRST NATIONAL BANK OF OMAHA • FIRST USA • FMC FULTS COMPANIES • FMF REALTY • FOOTHILLS CHURCH • FORD MOTOR COMPANY • GARDERE & WYNNE • GENERAL CORPORATION • GENERAL ELECTRIC • GIANT GROUP • GIVENCHY HOTEL & SPA • GLOBAL INDUSTRIES • GOLDCREST CONDOMINIUMS • GOLDMAN SACHS • GOVERNMENT OF ARGENTINA • GOVERNMENT OF THE KINGDOM OF SAUDIA ARABIA • GRAND CASINO COUSHATTA HOTEL • GRAND PRINCESS • GULFSTREAM • GREENPOINT SAVINGS BANK • GULF STATES TOYOTA • GULFSTREAM DEMONSTRATOR • HALL, DICKLER • HARBERT INTERNATIONAL • HARBOR COURT • HARRIS BANK • HARROD'S • HARVEY HOTEL • HEINZ USA • HENRI BENDEL • HERSHEY TRUST COMPANY • HEWLETT PACKARD • HOFFMAN LA ROCHE • HOLIDAY INN • HOUSTON DOUBLETREE GUEST SUITES • HOUSTONIAN HOTEL CLUB & SPA • HUDSON FOODS • IBM • INDIAN RIDGE • INGERSOLL RAND • INTERNATIONAL PAPER • ISK CONCERT HALL • ISLAND PRINCESS • ITT • JACKSON MISSISSIPPI AIRPORT OFFICES • JENNISON ASSOCIATES • JOHNSON & JOHNSON • JOHNSON PUBLISHING • JORDAN INDUSTRIES • J.P. MORGAN • JPI • KAPPA SIGMA FRATERNITY • KEY INVESTMENT • KK & R • KOCH INDUSTRIES • KONFARA • LA TOUR CONDOMINIUMS • LANCASTER HOTEL • LANGLEY FEDERAL CREDIT UNION • LASALLE PARTNERS • LATTICE • LAZARD FRERES • LIBERTY MUTUAL • BELL ATLANTIC • LIBERTY SPORTS • LIMITED • LINCOLN PROPERTY COMPANY • LINCOLN TOWERS • LITTLE NELL HOTEL • LOCKHEED ENGINEERING • LOUISIANA GOVERNOR'S MANSION • LUCASFILM • MARATHON OIL • MARRIOTT'S TAN-TAR-A-RESORT • MARRIOTT CUSTOM HOUSE HOTEL • MARY KAY COSMETICS • MASTERCARD • MAUNA LANI BAY • MCKINSEY & COMPANY • MCKOY PEAK LODGE • MCWANE COMPANIES • MEADOWBROOK CARE CENTER • MEDPARTNERS • MERCK • MERRILL LYNCH • MET LIFE • MILBANK, TWEED, HADLEY & MCCLOY • MILLER-BOYETT PRODUCTIONS • MONTGOMERY ASSET MANAGEMENT • MUSEUM OF SCIENCE AND INDUSTRY • MUTUAL OF AMERICA • NATIONS BANK • NEW YORK STATE DORMITORY AUTHORITY • NEW YORK STOCK EXCHANGE • NEWS CORPORATION • NIKE • NOMURA SECURITIES • NORTHWOOD CLUB • OAKTREE CAPITAL MANAGEMENT • OFFIT BANK • OLYMPIC AIRWAYS • OMNI ROYAL ORLEANS • ORACLE NASHUA • OXY CHEM • PACIFIC PRINCESS • PACIFIC TELESIS • PAGENET CORPORATION • PAN AMERICAN LIFE • PAUL STUART CHICAGO • PEBBLE BEACH COMPANY • PEPSICO • PETROLA HOUSE • PFIZER • PHILLIP MORRIS • PORT AUTHORITY OF NEW YORK AND NEW JERSEY • PRESBYTERIAN HOSPITAL DALLAS • PROTECTIVE LIFE INSURANCE COMPANY • PULSAR • QUAIL CREEK GOLF & COUNTRY CLUB • QUANTAS AIRLINES • QUAKER RIDGE COUNTRY CLUB • REESE DESIGN INTERNATIONAL • REESE DESIGN LIMITED • REGENT NEW YORK • REYNOLDS & REYNOLDS • RITZ-CARLTON • RITZ-CARLTON, SAVANNAH • RODEN & HAYES • ROUSE & COMPANY • ROYAL PRINCESS • SAFRA NATIONAL BANK • S.M. PHELPS REALTY • SANFORD C. BERSTEIN & COMPANY INC. • SANTA MONICA BANK • SAUDI ROYAL FLIGHT • SEA PRINCESS • SEAFLITE • SEAGRAM'S • SHAW COMMUNICATIONS • SILBER PEARLMAN • SILVER STAR CASINO • SINCLAIR OIL COMPANY • SKADDEN, ARPS, SLATE, MEAGHER & FLOM • SKIDMORE OWINGS & MERRILL • SKOKIE COUNTRY CLUB • SOCIETE GENERAL • SODA UNIVERSITY OF AMERICA • SONY MUSIC • SOROS FUND MANAGEMENT • SOUTHERN CALIFORNIA GAS COMPANY • SOUTHERN HILLS COUNTRY CLUB • SOUTHERN STAR • ST. LUKE'S EPISCOPAL CHURCH • STAR PRINCESS • STATE OF NEBRASKA GOVERNOR'S MANSION • STERLING SOFTWARE • SUNSET CLUB • SWISS BANK CORPORATION/SWISS RE • T.X.I. • TENNESSEE VALLEY AUTHORITY • TEXTRON • THE BREVOORT • TORRAY • TRAVELERS GROUP • TRITON • TROPWORLD HOTEL • TRUST INVESTMENTS • TURTLE CREEK CENTRE • TWO ALLEN CENTER • TW UNION SQUARE • U.S. AIR • U.S. DEPT. OF STATE • U.S. SURGICAL • U.S. TRUST • U.S.F. & G. • UNION PACIFIC RESOURCES • UNITED SAUDI COMMERCIAL BANK • UNIVERSITY OF ALABAMA, BRUNO LIBRARY • UNIVERSITY OF CHICAGO • UNIVERSITY OF MICHIGAN RARE BOOKS • USX • UNITED STATES EMBASSY (CARACAS) • UNITED STATES EMBASSY (SINGAPORE) • VAIL CASCADE HOTEL • VALERO CORPORATE SERVICES COMPANY • VITRO • WALT DISNEY WORLD • WEBSTER BANK • WEIL GOTSHAL & MANGES • WELLS FARGO • WESTINGHOUSE • WESTSIDE LEXUS • WHITE & CASE • THE WHITE HOUSE • WILLIAMS SQUARE, LAS COLINAS • WOMEN'S ATHLETIC CLUB OF CHICAGO • WOODMARK HOTEL • WORLD BANK • WORLD SAVINGS BANK • WUNSCH/MCREADY • WYNDHAM HOTELS

BOSTON • CHICAGO • DALLAS • HOUSTON • DANIA • LOS ANGELES • NEW YORK • SAN FRANCISCO

http://www.dir-dd.com/edward-fields.html/

The executives, employees and customers of
work and walk on carpet by
EDWARD FIELDS
212-310-0400
232 EAST 59th ST • NEW YORK, NY 10022

serotina NuVo

HARDENcontract

SCHUMACHER.
CONTRACT
™

FABRICS, TRIMMINGS, WALLPAPERS & FURNISHINGS FOR CONTRACT & HOSPITALITY 1 800 572 0032

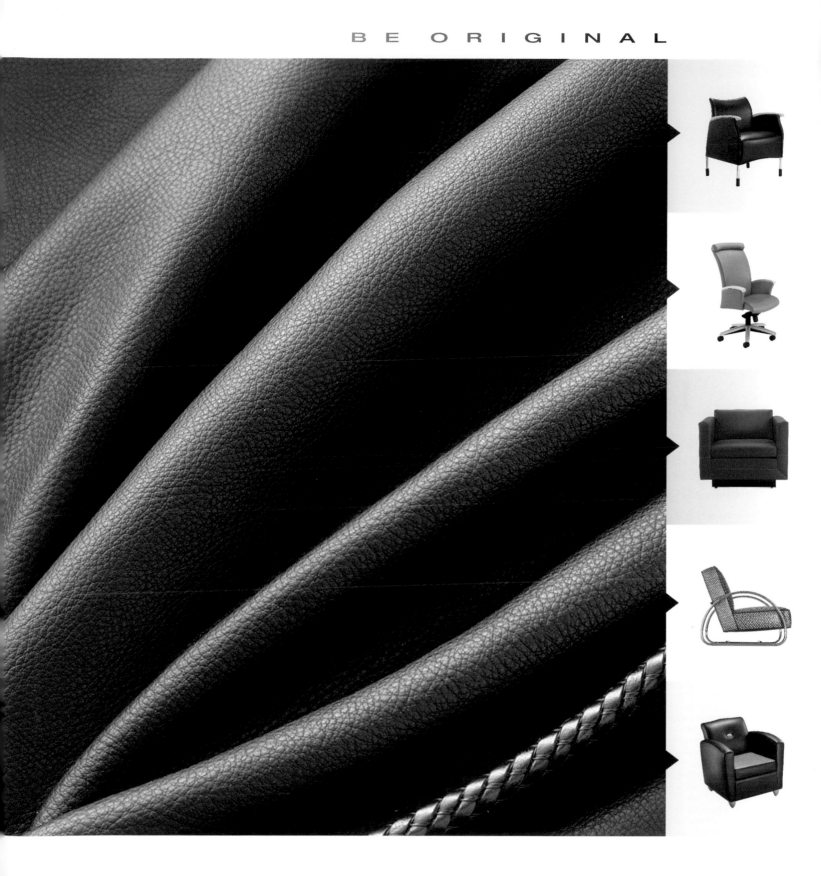

CALYPSO

DESIGN QUALITY SERVICE

Architectural Response Kollection, Inc.

www.ark-inc.com
toll free 888 241 7100
email info@ark-inc.com

GREAT PRODUCTS DON'T NEED TAGLINES

Cᴏɴsᴛᴀɴᴛɪɴᴇ

CONSTANTINE COMMERCIAL 800.308.4344

| Style: | Bob's Shirt | Pile Height: | 0.2 |
| Construction: | Patterned Cut & Loop | Width: | 12' |

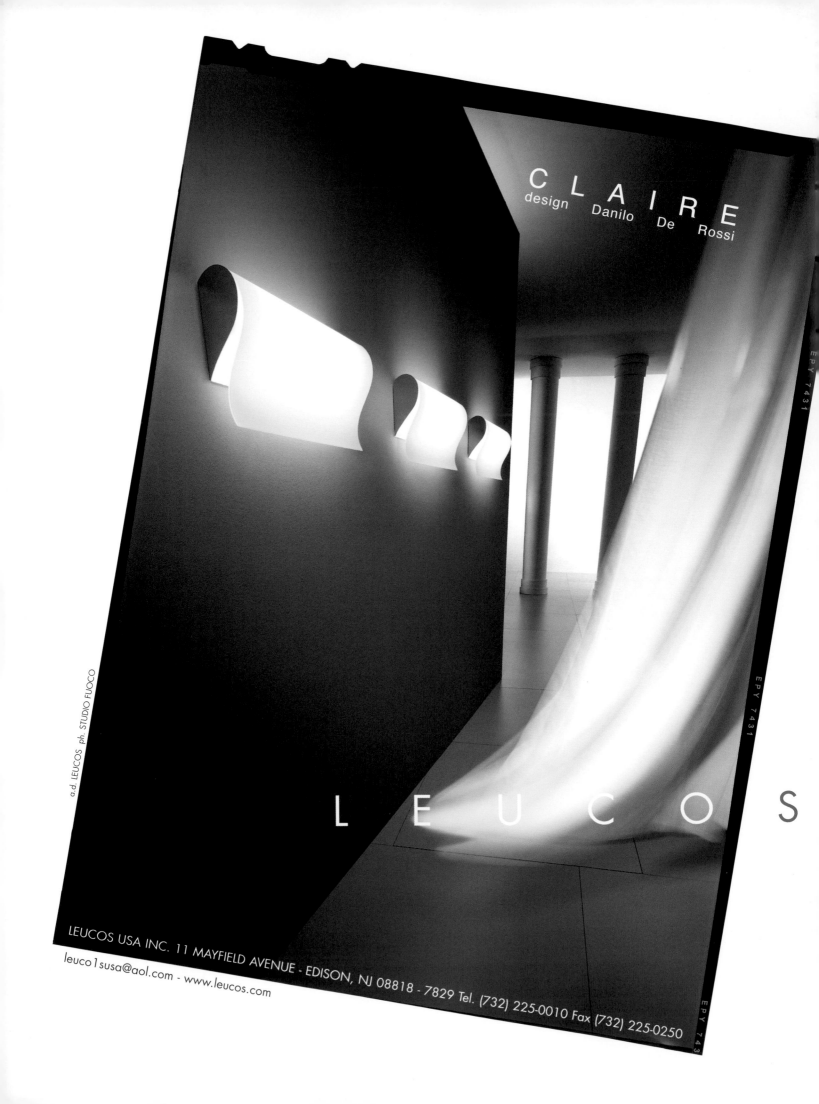

CLAIRE
design   Danilo   De   Rossi

a.d. LEUCOS ph. STUDIO FUOCO

LEUCOS

LEUCOS USA INC. 11 MAYFIELD AVENUE - EDISON, NJ 08818 - 7829 Tel. (732) 225-0010 Fax (732) 225-0250

leuco1susa@aol.com - www.leucos.com

EPY 7431

EPY 7431

EPY 743

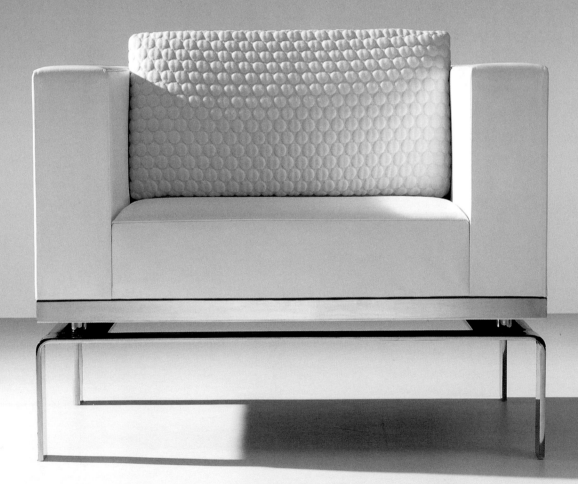

GRAFIK Eye®

Control all your lights

at the touch of a button...

...with Lutron's Grafik Eye Preset Lighting Controls

Lutron's Grafik Eye makes it easy to control all the lights in a single room or throughout a building so that any area can be used for multiple purposes. Set one button to create a bright atmosphere for a business gathering, another for a social occasion. All preset scenes can be easily recalled by pushing a single button.

Grafik Eye puts you in control.

For a free project analysis or instructional video and literature, contact the Lutron corporate headquarters at 1-877-2LUTRON (1-877-258-8766), ext 1000, or visit our website at www.lutron.com/corporateinteriors.

Innovations in Lighting Control

NeoCon® SHOWS

NeoCon®
Shows

NeoCon®
World's Trade
Fair

IIDEX®/
NeoCon®
Canada

NeoCon®
East

NeoCon®
West

North America's largest collection of expositions and conferences for interior design and facilities management ...

NeoCon® World's Trade Fair
June 14-16, 2004
The Merchandise Mart • Chicago, Ill.

IIDEX®/NeoCon® Canada
September 18-19, 2003
The National Trade Centre
Toronto, Ont.

NeoCon® East
November 6-7, 2003
Baltimore Convention Center
Baltimore, Md.

NeoCon® West
February 4-5, 2004
Los Angeles Convention Center
Los Angeles, Calif.

www.merchandisemart.com 800.677.6278

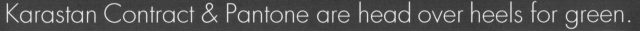

Karastan Contract & Pantone are head over heels for green.

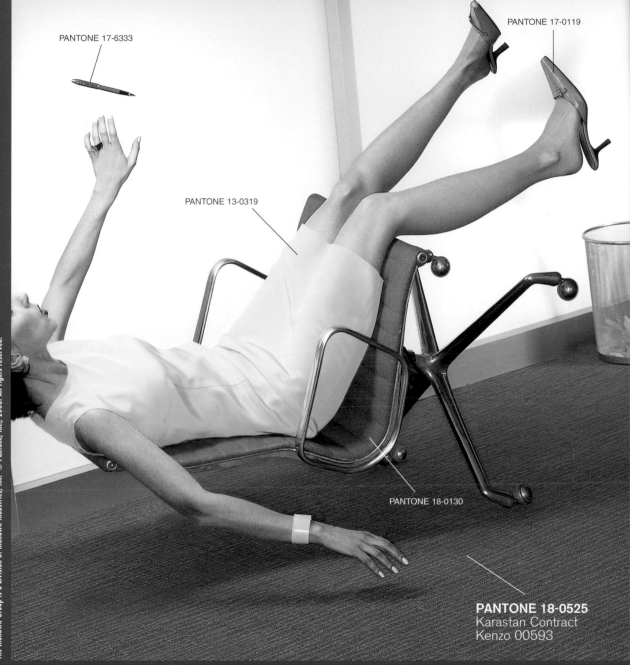

PANTONE 17-6333

PANTONE 17-0119

PANTONE 13-0319

PANTONE 18-0130

PANTONE 18-0525
Karastan Contract
Kenzo 00593

The Mohawk Group, a leading manufacturer of commercial carpeting, has formed a partnership with Pantone, the company that created a global color language. Now, contract and hospitality designers and specifiers can put their own spin on the latest color by using the system that the entire industry is falling for.

The Designtex Group Design. Evolve. Solve.

DESIGN
TEX
JM Lynne
Blumenthal
ESSEX™
Commercial Wallcovering
Lumicor®
loophouse

sit in design...

LIPSE Chair Series
designed by Wolfgang C.R. Mezger

...design *is* a choice

best of
NeoCon 2002
Gold
Winner

DAVIS

Davis Furniture Ind. Inc.
Tel 336 889 2009
Fax 336 889 0031
www.davisfurniture.com